MW01381215

10 MINUTE GUIDE TO

HTML STYLE SHEETS

by Craig Zacker

A Division of Macmillan Computer Publishing
201 West 103rd St., Indianapolis, Indiana 46290 USA

Library of Congress Catalog No.: 96-71434

ISBN: 0-7897-1034-x

99 98 97   6 5 4 3 2 1

Interpretation of the printing code: the rightmost double-digit number is the year of the book's printing; the rightmost single-digit number, the number of the book's printing. For example, a printing code of 97-1 shows that the first printing of the book occurred in 1997.

Printed in the United States of America

President Roland Elgey

Publisher Joseph B. Wikert

Editorial Services Director Elizabeth Keaffaber

Managing Editor Sandy Doell

Title Manager Mark Cierzniak

Acquisitions Editor Stephanie J. McComb

Product Director Benjamin Milstead

Editor Judy Ohm

Technical Editor Bill Bruns

Acquisitions Coordinator Jane K. Brownlow

Book Designer Barbara Kordesh

Cover Designer Dan Armstrong

Production Team Tricia Flodder, Janelle Herber, Daniela Raderstorf, Laure Robinson, Christy Wagner

Indexer Robert Long

CONTENTS

INTRODUCTION

HTML style sheets are a new innovation in World Wide Web development even though the concept of grouping document formatting elements into styles has been a staple of the desktop publishing industry for years. Applying styles to your HTML documents provides you with a wealth of new design possibilities for your web pages without resorting to the large graphic files that make many sites slow and unwieldy.

With HTML styles, you can be certain that your readers will see the text of your web pages exactly as you have designed it. The text and layout control capabilities that have previously been specified by the browser are returned to the author, where they belong.

At this time, there are only a handful of World Wide Web browsers that support the use of HTML style sheets. Version 3.0 of Microsoft's Internet Explorer is widely popular, freely available, and includes support for styles. Version 2 of Internet Explorer, however, which ships with the Windows 95 and Windows NT 4.0 operating systems, does not.

Currently, the only other browser capable of displaying documents with style sheets on the Windows platform is called Gnuscape Navigator. This is a port from a UNIX browser that requires you to install a large EMWACS emulator before it runs. Netscape, however, has announced that Version 4 of Netscape Navigator, which is scheduled for beta release before the end of 1996, will support styles.

This Netscape release will put support for style sheets into the two browsers that comprise the vast majority of the market share. However, even if readers use another browser to view your pages, the use of style sheets will not compromise your HTML code in any way. Browsers that don't support style sheets ignore the style codes and display your text in the usual way.

Obtaining Internet Explorer 3.0

Before you perform the activities in any of the lessons in this book, download Internet Explorer 3.0 and install it on your Windows 95 or Windows NT 4 PC—it is free of charge. If you are already using another web browser or an earlier version of Internet Explorer, use it to connect to Microsoft's web site at **http://www.microsoft.com/ie/download** and follow the instructions to download Explorer 3.0.

The file that you download to your machine is an executable **.exe** file. Select Run from the Windows Start menu and enter the name of the downloaded file along with its full path (for example, **C:\temp\msie30.exe**). Click OK to start the installation process. Follow the instructions provided by the setup screens to complete the browser installation. Be sure to click the HTML Layout Control checkbox when the installation program prompts you to select the browser options to be installed.

Microsoft has also released a patch for the Internet Explorer that resolves some relatively minor authentication and security issues. It is available from the same web page as the Explorer and should be installed by all users.

Once Internet Explorer 3.0 installs, familiarize yourself with its controls. If you are a previous user of Netscape Navigator, you will find that Explorer's operation is quite similar.

Working with HTML Code

Because HTML styles are a new innovation, tools have not yet been created to automate their creation and use. To learn about styles, you must work directly with the HTML code that comprises a web page. This book assumes that you are already familiar with the rudimentary procedures to create and modify an HTML document by manually editing the code.

This does not mean that you have to be a professional web site designer to use this book; however, experience creating web pages with editing tools like Netscape Navigator Gold that insulate the user from the actual HTML tags that define the document, does not prepare you for the task of adding styles to your pages.

If you have not worked with HTML at the code level, or if you simply want to brush up your knowledge, the *10 Minute Guide to HTML* (ISBN 0-7897-0541-9) is a good place to start. It explains the coding involved in creating the basic HTML page.

How To Use This Book

The lessons in this book contain exercises that show you how to take an existing web page, modify some aspect of the code, and then view the results in the browser. To do this, you need to run a text editor in addition to the Internet Explorer. Windows 95 and Windows NT both contain Notepad, a basic text editor, which is sufficient for these purposes. If you select the Source option from the View menu of Internet Explorer, the browser opens Notepad and loads the document that is currently displayed in the browser.

If you wish, you may utilize any other text editor as long as it can save files in plain text (or ASCII) format.

Selecting a Text Editor   There are many hybrid web authoring tools available that fall somewhere between a WYSIWYG editor (like Netscape Navigator that displays no HTML tags) and a plain text editor (that displays all of the HTML code as text). Do not use these applications to perform the exercises in this book. Always avoid editors that attempt to check documents for correct HTML coding. The syntax used by HTML styles is too new to be supported by these tools and false error reports are likely to result.

Whatever text editor you use, you should be familiar with the procedure for switching between two applications in the Windows environment. Using key combinations like ALT+TAB or

ALT+ESC to switch between editor and browser is the fastest way to perform steps that you will repeat many times. ALT+TAB enables you to switch back to the most recently used application on your system (even if more than two are running), whereas ALT+ESC cycles through all of the open applications on the system in a preset order.

For the lessons in this book, the basic exercise technique is to modify HTML code in the text editor, save the changes to a file on a local drive, and then load the newly saved file into the Explorer web browser. You should try to become accustomed to the rhythm of saving your changes in the editor, switching to the browser, and using the F5 key or the CTRL+R combination to reload the browser display. As you gain speed, you will soon find yourself concentrating more on the effects of your modifications rather than on the mechanics themselves.

TIP **Using Wordpad**   Notepad lacks a hot key for the File Save command so you may want to use the Wordpad application that comes with Windows 95 and Windows NT. You also must remember to save your HTML files as text documents, enclosing the file name in quotes to prevent a **.txt** extension from being added to them. The CTRL+S key combination in Wordpad saves your changes to the open file.

Where Do I Start?

The lessons in this book take a simple HTML file and systematically modify it to demonstrate the design and layout capabilities of HTML styles.

Although it is not essential that you run through all of the lessons or read them in the order in which they appear, you should definitely begin with Lessons 1 through 4. These lessons present the basic method for defining and applying HTML styles. Lessons 5 and 6, and 18–20 show which styles can be applied to specific parts of a document. If you wish, you can begin to study any or all of the text and layout properties covered in lessons 7–17.

Keep in mind that the HTML code used in a lesson often builds on the modifications made in the preceding lesson. If you choose to skip lessons, be sure that your sample file contains the exact code that appears in each example. Otherwise, the results that you see in your browser may not be the same as those shown in the figures of the book.

Conventions Used in This Book

You'll find icons throughout this book to help you save time and learn important information:

 **Timesaver Tips**   These give you insider hints for using HTML styles more efficiently.

 **Plain English**   These icons call your attention to definitions of new terms.

 **Panic Button**   Look to these icons for warnings and cautions about potential problem areas.

You'll also find common conventions for steps you will perform:

What you type	Things you type will appear in bold, color type.
Press Enter	Any keys you press or items you select with your mouse will appear in color type.

On-screen text	Any on-screen messages you will see will appear in bold type.
New terms	New terms will appear in italic.
Press Alt+F1	Any key combinations you press will appear in this format.

Trademarks

All terms mentioned in this book that are known to be trademarks have been appropriately capitalized. Que Corporation cannot attest to the accuracy of this information. Use of a term in this book should not be regarded as affecting the validity of any trademark or service mark.

Screen reproductions in this book were created by means of the program Collage Plus from Inner Media, Inc., Hollis, NH.

Adding "Style" to Your Web Pages

In this lesson, you learn how styles can improve the appearance, readability, and manageability of your web pages.

A style is a collection of text and layout attributes that can be selectively applied to all or part of a document. These attributes can include font selection, font size and weight, margins, indentations, leading, and other properties that affect the appearance of text on the page. Grouping them into a style allows the author to easily apply the same collection of attributes to many different parts of a document.

Styles, as applied to HTML documents, provide web page designers with many advantages:

- Greater author control over appearance of text and its placement on the page

- Reduced clutter of multiple opening and closing tags on individual text elements

- Simplified modification of page design through style editing

- Elimination of the need for clumsy HTML workarounds to achieve basic layout effects

- Great improvement of the design potential for HTML pages without introducing a large number of new proprietary tags, or compromising the ability of other browsers to effectively display the document text.

If you want to have section headings with a different font than the regular text, in a larger size, and in italics, you normally would have to perform three distinct formatting tasks for each of the headings. With styles, you would only have to create a single style definition consisting of the three desired font attributes and then apply it to each of the headings.

Styles also reduce the clutter of your HTML pages by reducing the number of tags that are needed to create a particular effect. To achieve the desired effect for the headings described above using normal HTML tags, you would have to change this line of code:

```
<H2>This is a Headline</H2>
```

to this one:

```
<H2><FONT FACE="ARIAL" SIZE=5><B><I>This is a Headline
</I></B></FONT></H2>
```

for all of the headings in the document. HTML styles allow you to actually change the default behavior of standard tags like <H2>. By assigning a style to the <H2> tag that calls for Arial, size 5, and bold italic type, no changes have to be made to the headline coding at all.

In addition to the savings in time and effort gained in applying formatting to text, styles also make it much easier to modify your designs once they are applied. To change the appearance of all of the headlines to which you have applied a style, simply change the style definition itself and all of the headlines change. This makes it easier to experiment with different design ideas and readily see the results of your efforts.

Styles have been a common tool in word processing and page layout programs for many years, but they are only now being developed for use in HTML documents.

THE DEFAULT BROWSER STYLE

HTML style sheets are innovative primarily because they allow various styles to be applied to web pages by the author. All web browsers already use a default style to display text.

Most web browsers allow the user to modify the way in which text displays on the screen. All versions of Netscape Navigator and Microsoft Internet Explorer allow you to select background colors and the type and color of the font. The default style for the Internet Explorer on the Windows platform, for example, displays black Times New Roman text on a blue background, as shown in Figure 1.1. These attributes can be overridden by settings specified in the HTML code itself.

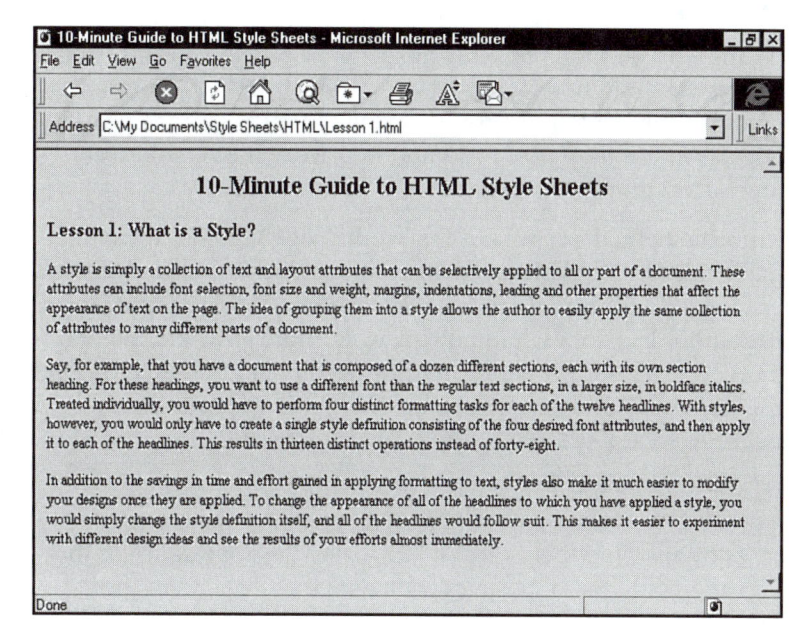

FIGURE 1.1   The appearance of a web page's text in any browser is the default style of that browser.

This display is, in fact, using a style. As described earlier, you can globally change the appearance of a document by modifying settings in the web browser to select a different font, a different text background color, or even a different default text size. This allows the browser to be customized to the user's preference and accommodates the needs of different sized screens or users with vision difficulties.

Two fundamental problems exist with the default browser style. It is a single style that must be universally applied to all documents and it is completely under the control of the user. As a result, authors have little or no say regarding many aspects of the appearance of text in their web pages.

AUTHOR STYLES VERSUS READER STYLES

People with desktop publishing experience often express frustration at the limitations imposed upon them by HTML. They are used to a tremendous degree of flexibility that allows them to select from thousands of fonts and to place text or graphics at precise locations on the page.

Unfortunately, the nature of the World Wide Web has thus far made this kind of design flexibility impossible. A web browser can only use the fonts that are installed on the user's computer, and the author has no way of knowing what those fonts are. What's more, the page on which the author's document presents (that is, the browser window), can be adjusted to any size so the document must be able to conform to the chosen size.

HTML style sheets are the result of an effort to return a greater amount of these fundamental design decisions to web page authors by allowing them more control over the appearance of the text and white space in their documents that displays in the reader's web browser.

 **White Space** White space is an expression used by page layout artists to describe all of the area on any color page that is not covered by text or other elements. It can include margins on all four sides of a page, paragraph indentations, and even the space between lines of text.

HTML DESIGN WORKAROUNDS

In an effort to overcome the design limitations imposed by the HTML language, many web page authors have come up with their own *workarounds*. They have invented ways to use HTML tags in ingenious ways to achieve particular ends. You can, for example, surround a paragraph with one or more <OL> or <UL> tags to create a left indent or use <BLOCKQUOTE> tags to indent on both sides. The use of borderless tables is now a standard means of providing some page layout flexibility.

These techniques are useful and often ingenious, but they are usually quite clumsy. They provide a given effect but with a very limited amount of control. You may have to "unlearn" these techniques when you create HTML documents using styles. In addition, adapting existing HTML documents to use styles may require the removal of the nonstandard tags, especially if you intend to save your style sheets as separate files and apply them to multiple HTML documents.

HTML styles enable much more control over the effects they provide than any other method of HTML coding. By the use of absolute or relative values, precise measurements of margins, indents, and other white space elements are possible.

The CSS1 Standard

The HTML styles in Microsoft's Internet Explorer 3.0 are based on a draft standard being developed by the World Wide Web Consortium (W3C), an independent body devoted to the creation and development of open web standards. The specification, called *Cascading Style Sheets, Level 1* (or CSS1), is still to be considered a work-in-progress, but the basic conception and syntax for the application of style sheets to HTML documents is complete.

You can examine the current version of the CSS1 draft standard at the World Wide Web Consortium's web site at **http://www.w3.org/pub/WWW/TR**.

Although Internet Explorer 3.0 is currently the only major web browser to support HTML style sheets, Netscape has committed to supporting style sheets in its Navigator 4.0 release in early 1997.

Another advantage of HTML styles (as defined in the CSS1 standard) is that the new codes used to define the styles do not affect the appearance of an HTML document in a browser that doesn't support styles. A web page with applied styles is still readable in any browser.

Because the CSS1 standard is in development, the style sheet support provided in Internet Explorer 3.0 differs from the standard in several ways, as follows:

- **Unsupported Properties**   Several of the controls defined in the standard have not yet been realized.

- **Erratic Backgrounds**   The application of background images using the various types of styles produces unpredictable results.

- **Margin Control**   The margins of adjacent documents' elements are not inherited and collapse in the manner described by the standard.

Some of the features that have not yet been realized in this version of the browser are included in this book for the sake of completion and adherence to the standard, and they are identified as such in the lessons.

TYPES OF STYLE SHEETS

HTML styles can be applied to web pages in three different ways:

- Linked
- Embedded
- Inline

The syntax of the style definitions are basically the same for each of the three types. The style types can also be combined in a single document. It is the relationship between the types that results in the cascading effect mentioned in the title of the CSS1 standard. In Lesson 2, you learn to create embedded styles first because they introduce nearly all of the essential concepts that you need to use styles.

Linked and inline styles, as well as the mixing of style types, are covered in Lessons 18, 19, and 20. By that time, you will know how to use all of the basic text formatting properties and be ready to consider the bigger picture of your web site's documents as a whole.

Linking to a Style Sheet

The term *style sheet* implies that the styles are stored in a file that is separate from the actual content of the documents. An HTML file uses the <LINK> tag as a reference to the style sheet. When you use HTML style sheets in this manner, you store your styles in a central location and apply them to many different documents. Conversely, you can apply multiple style sheets to a single document and allow them either to create a cumulative effect or to provide a menu to the readers so they can select the style of their choice.

Embedding a Style Block

You can also include your styles within the individual documents to which they are applied. By embedding them within the <HEAD> tags of an HTML file, the styles remain invisible to the reader and can be applied to many different elements of a web page.

Using Inline Styles

Inline styles are included as attributes within the actual HTML tags of a document. This means that they affect only the single element to which they are applied. Inline styles defeat some of the major advantages of styles because they add more code and clutter to the body of the document instead of less. Some occasions call for you to apply a special style to a single element, and an inline style definition is the quickest and easiest way to do it.

In this lesson, you learned how HTML style sheets can help you create better web pages. In the next lesson, you learn the basic method for adding styles to HTML documents.

MODIFYING HTML TAG STYLES

In this lesson, you learn how to create styles in HTML documents that modify the effect of standard HTML tags.

Anyone who has created an HTML document is familiar with the standard effects produced by certain HTML tags. Headline tags are in boldface, list tags are indented, and so forth. With styles, you can actually modify the properties that are applied to your documents with the various HTML tags.

CREATING A SAMPLE DOCUMENT

Before creating and applying styles, you must have an HTML document to work with. To begin, open your text editor and create a simple HTML document containing at least two different levels of headlines and some paragraph text, as follows:

```
<HTML>
<HEAD>
<TITLE>10-Minute Guide to HTML Style Sheets</TITLE>
</HEAD>
<BODY>
<H1>Lesson 1</H1>
<P> A style is simply a collection of text and layout
attributes that can be selectively applied to all or part
of a document. The idea of grouping them into a style
allows the author to easily apply the same collection of
attributes to many different parts of a document.</P>
<H2>The CSS1 Standard</H2>
```

```
<P>The HTML styles in Microsoft's Internet Explorer 3.0
are based on a draft standard being developed by the
World Wide Web Consortium (W3C), an independent body
devoted to the creation and development of open web
standards.</P>
</BODY>
</HTML>
```

You can use any text you wish in the document as long as the HTML tags are the same. Once you are finished, save the document on your local hard drive as a file called **SAMPLE.HTML** (or any other file name you prefer) and load the file you have just created into the Internet Explorer, using the following procedure:

1. Launch the Internet Explorer browser.

2. Select Open from the File menu and click the Browse button.

3. Highlight the SAMPLE.HTML file in the standard Open dialog box presented and click the Open button.

4. Click OK.

TIP **Opening Files** Rather than use the File Open dialog box, you can simply locate the desired file in the Windows Explorer or the My Computer window and double-click it.

You should now see your HTML code in the text editor and also in your web browser, as shown in Figure 2.1.

Each time you make a change in the code, save your changes in the editor and then refresh the document in the browser by pressing the F5 key, typing **<CTRL>+R**, or selecting Refresh from the browser's View menu to view the results.

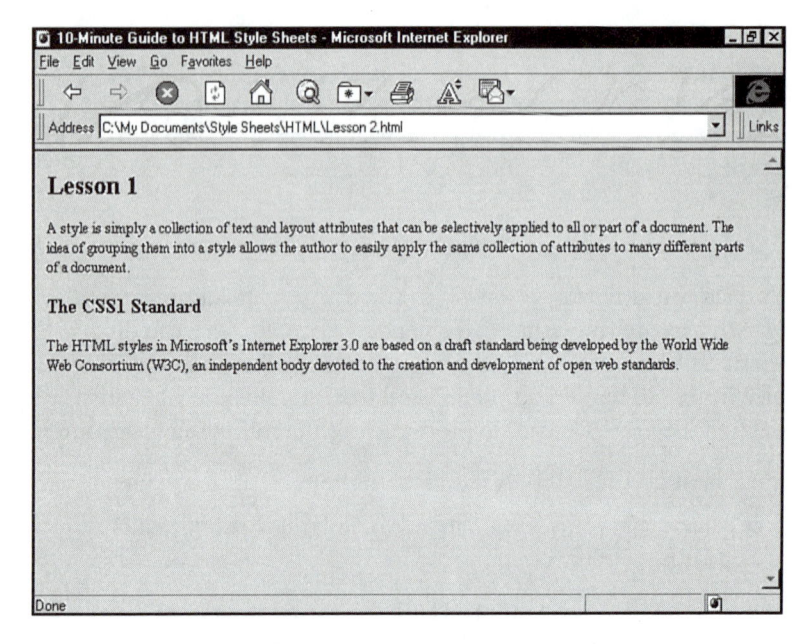

Figure 2.1   A basic web page using standard HTML codes will cause the browser's default style to be applied to the text.

Using the *<STYLE>* Tag

The creation of a style begins with the application of a new <STYLE> tag. When you are creating embedded styles in an HTML document, it is best to place the <STYLE> tag within the HEAD section of the document, that is, anywhere between the <HEAD> and </HEAD> tags. As is usually the case with HTML, you must have both an opening <STYLE> tag and a closing </STYLE> tag. Place the style definitions that you wish to embed in the document between these two tags.

The style definitions consist of three parts:

- Selectors
- Properties
- Values

A selector designates where a particular style definition is applied to an HTML document. In this lesson, the selectors are regular HTML tags whose default appearance will be modified. This is called a simple selector. A later lesson covers the creation of more complicated selectors.

TIP See Lesson 4, "Applying Styles with Class Selectors," and Lesson 5, "Using Contextual Selectors," for instruction on creating advanced selectors.

Within the opening and closing `<STYLE>` tags, each selector is specified on a separate line followed by the properties and values that are to be assigned to that selector.

SPECIFYING STYLE PROPERTIES AND THEIR VALUES

A property is one of the general parameters that a style can apply to the parts of an HTML document. Properties can be indicated by a particular selector, such as font size, color, or text alignment. A value is assigned to each property to define the precise nature of the parameter to be applied. For example, the `font-size` property may have a value of 16 points and the color parameter may have a value of black, red, or blue. The combination of a property and its value is called a *rule*.

The properties that are to be assigned to a particular selector always begin on the same line as the selector with at least one space between them. You enclose the properties in curly brackets and separate them with semicolons. Separate properties from their values with colons.

TIP Complete discussions of all the style properties available and their possible values can be found in Lessons 7 through 17.

Adding a basic embedded style sheet with simple selectors and a few simple properties to the sample HTML document you created above, makes the file appear as follows:

```
<HTML>
<HEAD>
<TITLE>10-Minute Guide to HTML Style Sheets</TITLE>
<STYLE>
<!--
H1    {font-size: 24pt; color: red; text-align: center}

H2    {font-size: 20pt; font-style: italic; color: blue}
-->
</STYLE>
</HEAD>
<BODY>
<H1>Lesson 1</H1>
<P> A style is simply a collection of text and layout
attributes that can be selectively applied to all or part
of a document. The idea of grouping them into a style
allows the author to easily apply the same collection of
attributes to many different parts of a document.</P>
<H2>The CSS1 Standard</H2>
<P>The HTML styles in Microsoft's Internet Explorer 3.0
are based on a draft standard being developed by the
World Wide Web Consortium (W3C), an independent body
devoted to the creation and development of open web
standards.</P>
</BODY>
</HTML>
```

Notice that the only changes made to the document are within the <HEAD> tags. When you are using simple selectors, no change to the body of the document is needed.

Add the style definitions shown previously (the <STYLE> tags and everything in between) to your **SAMPLE.HTML** file and reload it into the Internet Explorer. You should see a display like the one shown in Figure 2.2

TIP **Adding Remarking Codes** You can place your <STYLE> tags and their enclosed definitions within the <BODY> tags of your document. Locating them in the <HEAD> section, however, ensures that the codes do not display as text when viewed in a browser that does not support style sheets. When locating styles in the body of a document, enclose the style definitions within remark codes (that is, <!-- before and --> after) as shown in the previous sample. A browser that doesn't support styles ignores the <STYLE> and </STYLE> tags, but will display the definitions themselves as paragraph text, unless instructed otherwise.

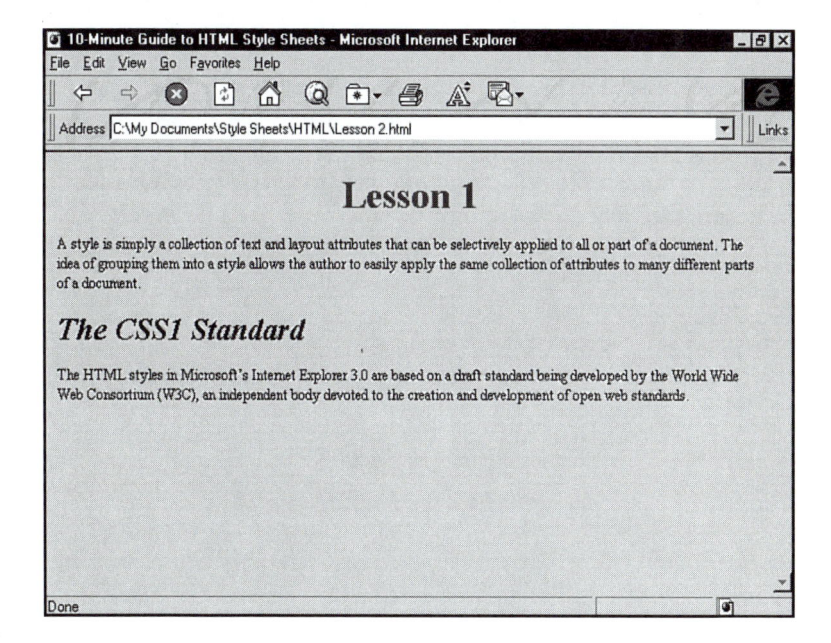

FIGURE 2.2   The addition of styles changes the appearance of the sample web page without altering any of the body code.

As you can see, the headlines increase in size and their color changes. The <H1> headline is now centered and the <H2> headline is italicized. Although no text-align property was specified for the H2 selector, the <H2> tag in the document retains the left-justification applied by the default browser style.

Styles behave in this way for all selectors and properties. Only the properties defined for a particular selector change in the document by the addition of the style. All other properties retain the values that they would normally possess.

You are, of course, not limited to the use of headline tags as simple selectors. You can apply style definitions to any existing HTML tag to change its appearance in the browser. You can apply style properties to an entire document by using the <BODY> tag as a selector, or to a single word or character using tags like <STRONG> and <EM>.

In this lesson, you learned the basic technique for embedding a style in an HTML document. In the next lesson, you add more styles to your sample document and see how the styles assigned to different parts of a document interact with each other.

UNDERSTANDING STYLE INHERITANCE

In this chapter, you learn how styles applied to particular HTML elements are passed down to the tags contained within them.

Applying styles to your documents effectively and efficiently requires an understanding of the rules by which styles affect the appearance of a document. One of the primary reasons for using styles is to reduce the amount of coding needed to achieve the desired effect. This can be done primarily because styles that are applied to one element of an HTML document are inherited by the other elements that fall between the tags.

Element   In HTML terms, an element is any part of an HTML document that can be distinguished from the whole of the document by reference to a particular HTML tag. For example, a paragraph element is contained between <P> tags. Tags that offset their content from other elements with line breaks (such as paragraphs and headlines) create *block level elements*. Tags that do not force line breaks (like <STRONG> and <B>) create *inline elements*.

If style properties were not inherited, it would be necessary for you to define the same properties over and over for many different selectors. You would be writing the same amount of code as if you were using traditional HTML tags for each individual element but storing the code in a different place.

To illustrate this, take your **SAMPLE.HTML** file from the end of Lesson 2 and add a style definition for the <BODY> tag. This creates a file that appears as follows:

```
<HTML>
<HEAD>
<TITLE>10-Minute Guide to HTML Style Sheets</TITLE>
<STYLE>
<!--
H1      {font-size: 24pt; color: red; text-align: center}

H2      {font-size: 20pt; font-style: italic; color: blue}

BODY     {font-family: Arial; background: yellow}
-->
</STYLE>
</HEAD>
<BODY>
<H1>Lesson 1</H1>
<P> A style is simply a collection of text and layout
attributes that can be selectively applied to all or part
of a document. The idea of grouping them into a style
allows the author to easily apply the same collection of
attributes to many different parts of a document.</P>
<H2>The CSS1 Standard</H2>
<P>The HTML styles in Microsoft's Internet Explorer 3.0
are based on a draft standard being developed by the
World Wide Web Consortium (W3C), an independent body
devoted to the creation and development of open web
standards.</P>
</BODY>
</HTML>
```

When you reload **SAMPLE.HTML** in the browser, you should see that the font for the entire document has changed from Times New Roman (the browser default) to Arial, and the background color has changed from the default light blue to yellow, as shown in Figure 3.1.

 **TIP** **Ordering Selectors**   Note that according to the CSS1 standard, the selectors within the <STYLE> tags can be listed in any order, as can the properties defined for any selector. In practice, however, Internet Explorer 3.0 sometimes behaves erratically when faced with certain combinations. If certain selectors or properties are not being recognized by the browser (and you are certain that they are coded correctly), try changing the order of the selectors or the properties for a given selector.

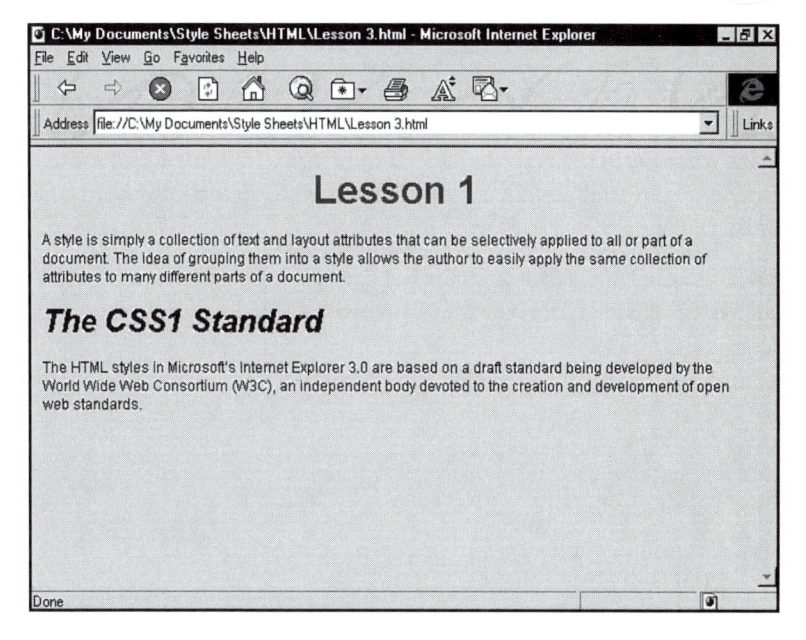

FIGURE 3.1 Style properties applied to the <BODY> tag are inherited by all of the other tags within the body of the document.

The font and the background color of the whole document are changed because the headline and paragraph elements are all contained within the <BODY> tags, and the properties applied to <BODY> are passed down. The <BODY> tag is the *parent* element and the headline and paragraph elements are the *children*.

This ancestral metaphor can be extended to encompass all of the elements in your HTML file. Most of the properties that you can include in a style sheet (but not all of them!) are inherited by the child elements of the selectors for which they are defined.

The background property is one that is not inherited. The entire background appears yellow in the above example because each selector in the style sheet is assigned a default background property of transparent that allows the <BODY> tag's defined yellow background color to show through.

LAYERING STYLES EFFECTIVELY

A good tag to use for style properties for most or all of a document is the <BODY> tag. You can still override the inherited <BODY> style for a particular child element by simply including the same properties in that element's style definition but with different values.

To illustrate this, add a selector for the <P> tag to your **SAMPLE.HTML** file, leaving you with a <STYLE> section that appears as follows:

```
<STYLE>
<!--
H1      {font-size: 24pt;
color: red;
text-align: center}

H2      {font-size: 20pt;
    font-style: italic;
    color: blue}

BODY     {font-family: Arial;
background: yellow}

P      {font-family: Times New Roman }
-->
</STYLE>
```

As a result, the browser display appears as shown in Figure 3.2.

Because the <P> tag has been explicitly assigned a value of Times New Roman, it no longer inherits the Arial value from the <BODY> tag, as the headlines do. In fact, the <P> sections start off with the browser's default font value of Times New Roman, change to Arial by the style assigned to the <BODY> tag, and change back to Times New Roman by the style applied to the <P> tag itself.

In some cases, coding your styles so that the same properties are redefined in this way is impractical and inefficient. At other times, it can be quite a time-saving technique. The logic by which you apply styles must be based on the nature of the document.

If the document in the above example had dozens of elements of various types (all using the Arial font except for the paragraphs), it would be easier to assign `font-family` properties to just the `<BODY>` and `<P>` tags than it would be to assign `Arial` to a dozen different elements.

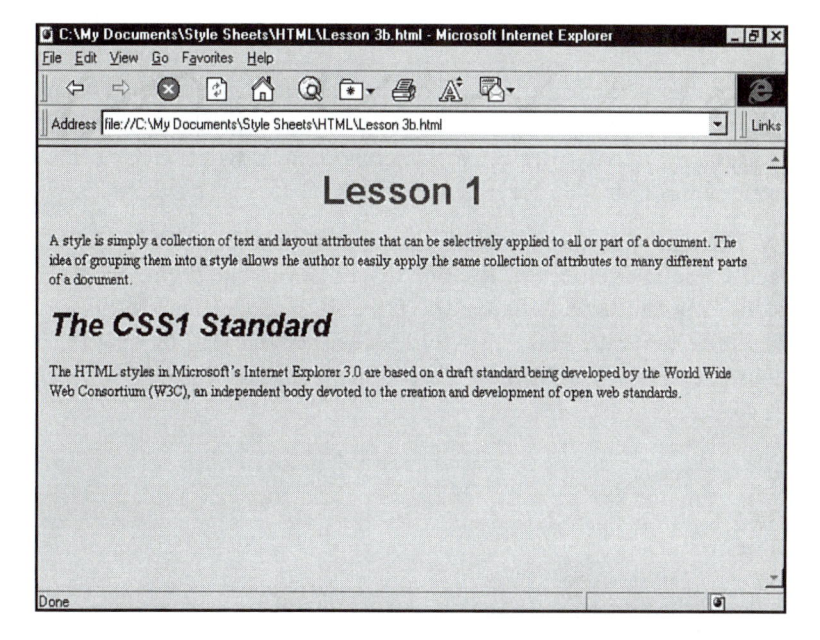

FIGURE 3.2 Property values are passed down from parent to child elements, except when they are overridden by the child's own assigned values.

Your goal should be to define as few properties as possible and keep your HTML code to the minimum needed to achieve the desired effect. The skillful use of selectors and the construction of HTML documents that lend themselves to your design needs are both habits that will develop. You learn skills later in this book that will enhance your capabilities.

RELATIVE VALUES

Style inheritance can also play an important role in the assignment of values to properties. As you will see in later lessons, many style properties can be assigned relative or absolute values.

Relative Value A relative value is one that is assigned by comparing it to the absolute value of its parent element.

In the examples used thus far, font sizes have been specified with the use of absolute values, measured in points. An absolute value causes a property to appear the same no matter what selector it is applied to or who its parents are.

For the next example, you will modify your **SAMPLE.HTML** file to use relative values for the font sizes of several elements in the form of percentages. Change the font-size properties for the headline elements and add a font-size property for the <BODY> element so that your <STYLE> section appears as follows:

```
<STYLE>
<!--
H1     {color: red;
    font-size: 200%;
    text-align: center}

H2     {font-size: 150%;
    font-style: italic;
    color: blue}

BODY    {font-family: "Arial";
    font-size: 150%;
    background: yellow}

P     {font-family: Times New Roman}
-->
</STYLE>
```

When you specify a relative value for a property that can be inherited, such as font size, the value that displays is computed by applying the percentage to the value of that property in its parent element. Thus, when you reload your modified **SAMPLE.HTML** file into the browser (see Figure 3.3), you see that all of the text is larger because the font size property for the <BODY> tag's style is defined as 150% of its parent element's font size.

The parent of the <BODY> element is the browser's default style so the font size of the body text in the sample is 150% of that shown in the earlier figures. Notice that the <H2> text that also has a

150% font size is larger than the body text. This is because the <H2> element's parent is the <BODY> element. When the font size for the <H2> text is computed, it is based on 150% of the parent element's actual size. The <H1> text is even larger because it is based on 200% of the same parent value as <H2>.

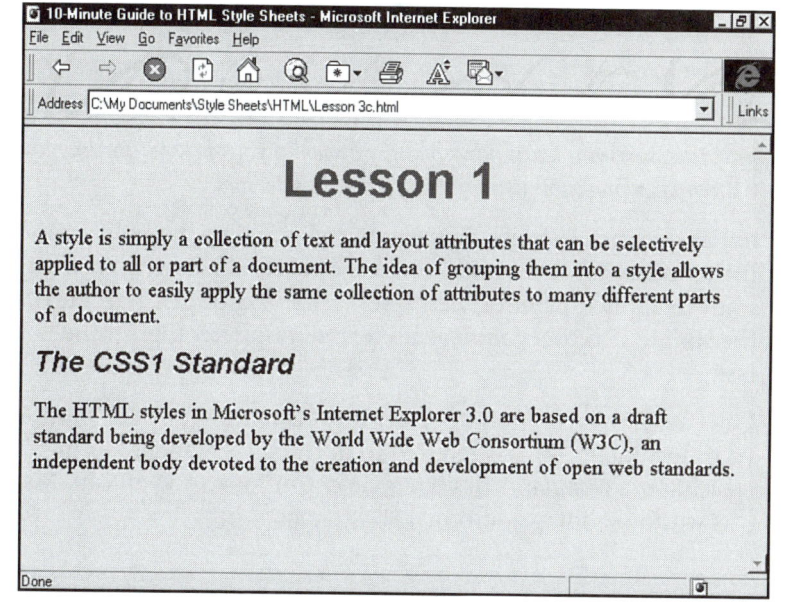

FIGURE 3.3 Relative values are based on the values inherited from the parent property.

This is a crucial part of understanding style inheritance. You will soon be applying styles to more complex HTML documents that have several generations of styles, each with relative values based on their ancestry. When you elect to use relative values, you must be aware of the way in which a small code change affects the appearance of elements several generations down the line.

In this lesson, you learned how styles can be inherited by the elements that are contained within other elements. In the next lesson, you create more complex selectors that you can use to assign styles to your documents with greater precision.

APPLYING STYLES WITH CLASS SELECTORS

In this lesson, you learn how to apply styles to your HTML documents with greater precision using more elaborate selectors.

In the previous lessons, you created styles and applied them to the familiar HTML tags that you use in every document. If you want to apply different styles to several blocks of paragraph text, the simple selectors you have used would not accomplish the task.

You can, however, apply style definitions to more specific parts of your documents. This is referred to in the CSS1 standard as increasing the *granularity* of your style definitions and you can do this without adding additional HTML tags.

Granularity   Granularity is the degree to which like elements in an HTML document have had individual styles applied to them through the use of distinguishing selectors.

USING THE *CLASS* ATTRIBUTE

To uniquely identify particular document elements that are bounded by the same HTML tags as other elements, you can apply different CLASS attributes to each one. Thus, if you have a document with several text blocks contained within <P> tags, you would modify the opening <P> tags to include the CLASS attribute and a variable to be used as an identifier for that paragraph, in the form <P CLASS=*variable*>.

 **Class** A class is simply a label, independent of any particular HTML tag, that is used to identify HTML elements to which a certain style will be applied.

Once you are able to identify specific paragraphs by their class, you can create style definitions for the individual classes. To illustrate this, modify your **SAMPLE.HTML** file from the previous lesson to appear as shown:

```
<HTML>
<HEAD>
<TITLE>10-Minute Guide to HTML Style Sheets</TITLE>
<STYLE>
<!--
H1      {font-size: 18pt; color: red; text-align: center}

H2      {font-size: 16pt; font-style: italic; color: blue}

BODY      {font-family: "Arial"; background: yellow}
-->
</STYLE>
</HEAD>
<BODY>
<H1>Lesson 1</H1>
<P CLASS=left> A style is simply a collection of text and
layout attributes that can be selectively applied to all
or part of a document. The idea of grouping them into a
style allows the author to easily apply the same
collection of attributes to many different parts of a
document.</P>
<H2>The Default Browser Style</H2>
<P CLASS=right>HTML style sheets are innovative primarily
in that they allow various different styles to be applied
to web pages by the author. Indeed, it could be said that
all web browsers already use a style to display text.</P>
<H2>The CSS1 Standard</H2>
<P CLASS=center>The HTML styles in Microsoft's Internet
Explorer 3.0 are based on a draft standard being
developed by the World Wide Web Consortium (W3C).</P>
</BODY>
</HTML>
```

Notice that an additional paragraph has been added and that the three paragraphs have been identified with classes labeled center, left, and right.

The names that are assigned to the classes are irrelevant—they simply have to match the styles that you create next.

If you reload **SAMPLE.HTML** into your browser at this time, you will see that the addition of the CLASS attributes did not affect the appearance of the page. This will also be true in other browsers that do not support the CSS1 standard. The document is still readable and appears as if the styles do not exist.

USING SPECIFIC CLASS SELECTORS

One way to apply a style to the classes that you have added is to create selectors that define the classes as variations of a particular HTML tag. A class selector always appears in the <STYLE> block with a period preceding it. Because you have already applied CLASS attributes called left, right, and center to the three <P> elements in the sample document, you will now create styles using class selectors named P.left, P.right, and P.center, as shown in the following modified <STYLE> block:

```
<STYLE>
<!--
H1     {font-size: 24pt;
        color: red;
        text-align: center}

H2     {font-size: 20pt;
        font-style: italic;
        color: blue}

BODY    {font-family: "Arial";
        background: yellow}

P.left      {margin-right=50%}

P.right     {margin-left=50%}

P.center      {margin-left=25%; margin-right=25%}
-->
</STYLE>
```

When you add these three new styles to your **SAMPLE.HTML** file and reload it into the browser, you see the results shown in Figure 4.1.

Ignoring the headlines, which have not been affected by these modifications, you can see that the addition of class identifiers allows the three paragraph elements to be placed in different areas of the canvas through the application of margin properties.

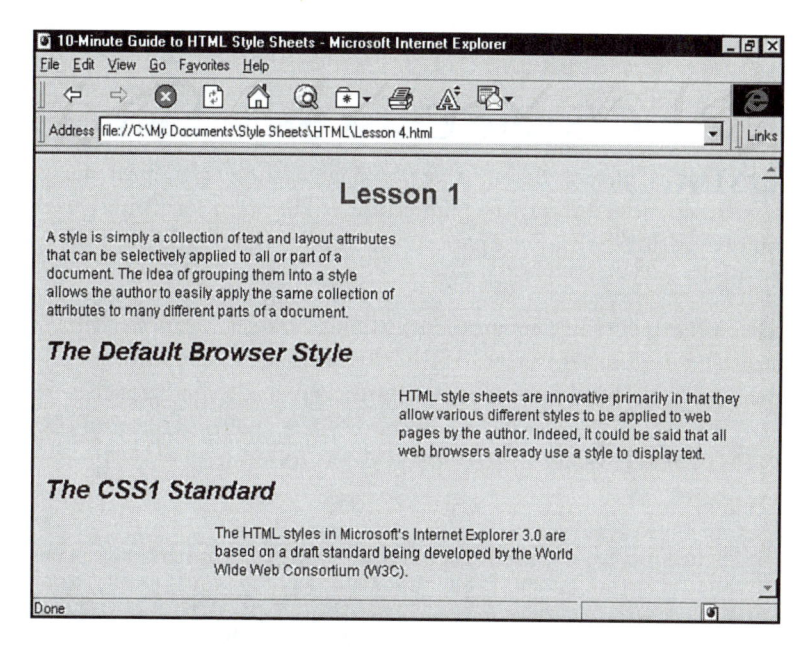

FIGURE 4.1 Class selectors allow you to apply different styles to HTML elements that use the same tag.

Canvas The term *canvas* is used by the CSS1 standard to define the space in the browser window on which HTML documents are actually displayed. The word is also used to imply that a greater degree of artistic control is provided by HTML styles, which allows text to be located on the browser screen with greater consistency and control.

Notice also that the application of classes has no effect on the inheritance of style attributes from the <P> tag's parent element. The Arial font and yellow background still pass down from the <BODY> tag's style as before.

The styles defined for the class selectors can contain any of the formatting properties that are defined in the CSS1 standard and supported by the browser. The use of selectors that address specific combinations of HTML tags and classes provides a wide range of design effects that enhance the appearance and flexibility of your web pages.

USING GENERIC CLASS SELECTORS

An obvious, glaring flaw in the web page is shown in Figure 4.1. You have moved the three paragraphs to different locations on the page, but their accompanying headlines have been left behind.

One way to correct this problem is to add classes to the headline tags just as you did earlier for the <P> tags. In fact, because the headlines are to be moved in the same way as the paragraphs, you can use the same class names to modify the <BODY> section of the **SAMPLE.HTML** document to appear as follows:

```
<BODY>
<H1 CLASS=left>Lesson 1</H1>
<P CLASS=left> A style is simply a collection of text and
layout attributes that can be selectively applied to all
or part of a document. The idea of grouping them into a
style allows the author to easily apply the same
collection of attributes to many different parts of a
document.</P>

<H2 CLASS=right>The Default Browser Style</H2>
<P CLASS=right>HTML style sheets are innovative primarily
in that they allow various different styles to be applied
to web pages by the author. Indeed, it could be said that
all web browsers already use a style to display text.</P>

<H2 CLASS=center>The CSS1 Standard</H2>
<P CLASS=center>The HTML styles in Microsoft's Internet
Explorer 3.0 are based on a draft standard being
developed by the World Wide Web Consortium (W3C).</P>
</BODY>
```

The CLASS attribute can be added to any HTML element to distinguish it from others with the same tag.

To complete the task, create specific class selectors for the headline tags called `H1.left`, `H2.right`, and `H2.center`. Then duplicate the style declarations that you created for the `P` selectors to achieve the desired result.

There is another type of class selector that makes this redundant coding unnecessary. Instead of precisely identifying all of the combinations of classes and elements and defining a separate style for each, you can create a generic selector for the class alone which is applied to any HTML element carrying that class attribute.

To do this, modify the `<STYLE>` block of the **SAMPLE.HTML** file again to appear as follows:

```
<STYLE>
<!--
H1      {font-size: 24pt;
        color: red;
        text-align: center}

H2      {font-size: 20pt;
        font-style: italic;
        color: blue}

BODY    {font-family: "Arial";
        background: yellow}

.left       {margin-right=50%}

.right      {margin-left=50%}

.center     {margin-left=25%;
        margin-right=25%}
-->
</STYLE>
```

Instead of adding to the style definitions, this time you simply removed the `P` from the three class selectors (leaving the periods) making them applicable to any HTML tag.

Save your changes, reload the file into the browser, and the desired effect is achieved (see Figure 4.2). The styles for the class selectors called `left`, `right`, and `center` are applied to all of the HTML tags (`<P>`, `<H1>`, and `<H2>`) containing their respective `CLASS` attributes.

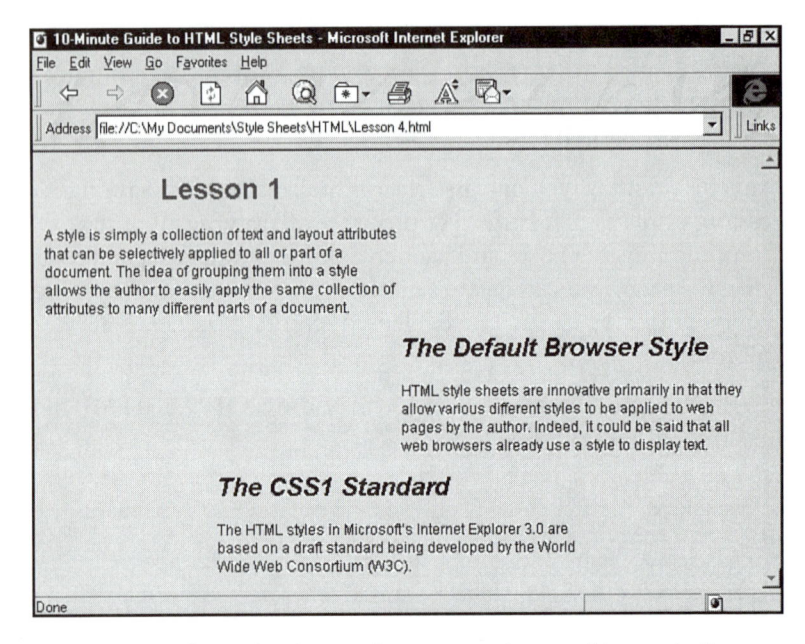

FIGURE 4.2   Generic class selectors can be used to apply the same style properties to any HTML element identified by that class.

Using these same selectors and style definitions, you could now apply the CLASS attributes to any HTML tag in the document and achieve the same effect for that element. Class selectors can be used to identify specific elements of a document, either in conjunction with, or wholly independent of, the HTML tags that define them.

In this lesson, you learned how to apply styles to specific areas of a web page using class selectors. In the next lesson, you create selectors with even greater precision.

Using Contextual Selectors

In this lesson, you learn how to assign styles to HTML tags based on the location of the tags within the hierarchy of your document.

In some cases, particularly when you are applying styles to existing HTML documents, you may want to apply styles with greater precision than that afforded by simple selectors and without having to add CLASS attributes through the body of the document. This can be done by using a particular HTML element as a selector and specifying that the style only be applied when that element is contained within another specific HTML element.

For example, you may want to change the color of the emphasized text in a document, but only within paragraphs, not in headlines. You can create a selector to assign a style rule to your document's <EM> tags, but only when they are enclosed within <P> tags. In the same way, you can have paragraph text that is smaller within table cells than it is outside a table, by assigning the smaller font size to <P> tags that fall within <TABLE> tags.

These are called *contextual selectors* because the style is applied to a tag based on its context within the document's HTML hierarchy.

A good way to illustrate this principle is with the use of the HTML codes that allow you to create lists. Create two lists, one ordered and one unordered, and add them to the beginning of the <BODY> block in your **SAMPLE.HTML** file, as follows:

```
<BODY>
<OL>
<LI>What is a style?</LI>
<LI>Modifying HTML Tag Styles</LI>
<LI>Understanding Style Inheritance</LI>
<LI>Using Class Selectors</LI>
```

```
<LI>Using Contextual Selectors</LI>
</OL>

<UL>
<LI>Greater author control over appearance of text and
its placement on the page
<LI>Reduced clutter of multiple opening and closing tags
on individual text elements
<LI>Simplified modification of page design through style
editing
<LI>Elimination of the need for clumsy HTML workarounds
to achieve basic layout effects
<LI>Great improvement of the design potential for HTML
pages without introducing a large number of new,
proprietary tags
</UL>
```

When loaded into the browser, **SAMPLE.HTML** now appears as shown in Figure 5.1.

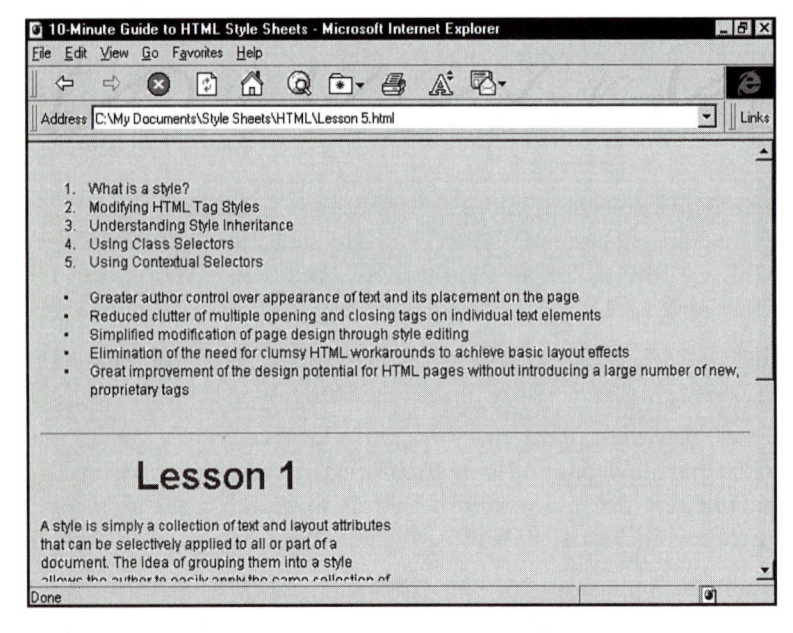

FIGURE 5.1   The ordered list code causes <LI> elements to be numbered; unordered lists, bulleted.

Now, assume that you want to apply different styles to the elements in each type of list. You could use class selectors to distinguish the <LI> tags in the ordered list from those of the unordered list, but you would have to add CLASS attributes to each tag. You might recall the rules of style inheritance and insert the CLASS attributes into the <OL> and <UL> tags instead, knowing that they would be carried down to the <LI> elements. This could be inconvenient if you want to apply your styles to a document with many lists or many documents with lists.

You can, instead, create styles with contextual selectors that identify the specific element to be stylized by citing its tag and its ancestry. A contextual selector is notated by specifying the tag for an HTML element, followed by the tag for another element contained inside the first, and separated by a space. Properties and values are then added in the usual manner. This forms a search stack. The entire search stack must be satisfied before the style is applied.

Modify the <STYLE> block of your **SAMPLE.HTML** file to add the OL LI and UL LI selectors, as shown:

```
<STYLE>
<!--
H1      {font-size: 24pt;
        color: red;
        text-align: center}

H2      {font-size: 20pt;
        font-style: italic;
        color: blue}

BODY    {font-family: "Arial";
        background: yellow}

.left      {margin-right: 50%}

.right      {margin-left: 50%}

.center      {margin-left: 25%; margin-right: 25%}

OL LI      {font-size: 125%;
        font-style: italic}

UL LI      {font-size: 75%;
        font-weight: bold}
-->
</STYLE>
```

When you save your changes and reload **SAMPLE.HTML** in the browser, you see that the ordered list's font is enlarged and italicized because its <LI> tags are contained within the <OL> tags (see Figure 5.2). The <LI> tags of the unordered list had a different style applied to them because their parent element is the <UL> tag.

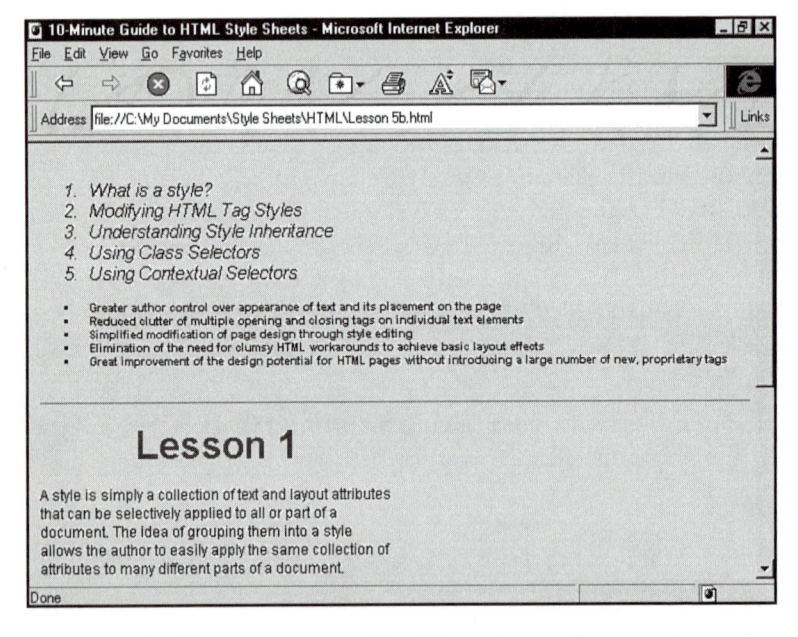

1. What is a style?
2. Modifying HTML Tag Styles
3. Understanding Style Inheritance
4. Using Class Selectors
5. Using Contextual Selectors

- Greater author control over appearance of text and its placement on the page
- Reduced clutter of multiple opening and closing tags on individual text elements
- Simplified modification of page design through style editing
- Elimination of the need for clumsy HTML workarounds to achieve basic layout effects
- Great improvement of the design potential for HTML pages without introducing a large number of new, proprietary tags

Lesson 1

A style is simply a collection of text and layout attributes that can be selectively applied to all or part of a document. The idea of grouping them into a style allows the author to easily apply the same collection of attributes to many different parts of a document.

FIGURE 5.2 The same tags with different parent elements can be assigned different styles using selectors that specify the tag's context.

USING THIRD-GENERATION SELECTORS

Selectors of even greater complexity are used in cases where several generations of HTML elements are present. In the next exercise, by combining the two lists created earlier into a single one, you achieve a multi-level outline effect in which the elements at the various levels are more easily distinguishable because of the different styles applied to each.

Modify **SAMPLE.HTML** to include the following ordered list in the <BODY> block:

```
<BODY>
<OL type=I>
<LI>What is a style?</LI>
<OL type=1>
<LI>Greater author control over appearance of text and
its placement on the page</LI>
</OL>
<LI>Modifying HTML Tag Styles</LI>
<OL type=1>
<LI>Elimination of the need for clumsy HTML workarounds
to achieve basic layout effects</LI>
<LI>Reduced clutter of multiple opening and closing tags
on individual text elements</li>
<OL type=i>
<LI>Simplified modification of page design through style
editing
<LI>Great improvement of the design potential for HTML
pages without introducing a large number of new,
proprietary tags
</OL>
<LI>Understanding Style Inheritance</LI>
</OL>
<LI>Using Class Selectors</LI>
<OL type=1>
<LI>Using Contextual Selectors</LI>
</OL>
</OL>
```

When you reload the file into the browser, the list appears as shown in Figure 5.3. All of the <LI> elements have the same style applied to them because the properties for the contextual selector OL LI are being applied to the elements at each level of the outline. This is because each <LI> tag has at least one <OL> tag as its ancestor.

TIP Notice that the numbering of the elements at each level of the outline is varied by the use of the TYPE attribute in the <OL> tags. This not only improves the readability of the outline in the browser, but also helps the author to keep track of the often confusing layers of <OL> and <LI> tags in the HTML code.

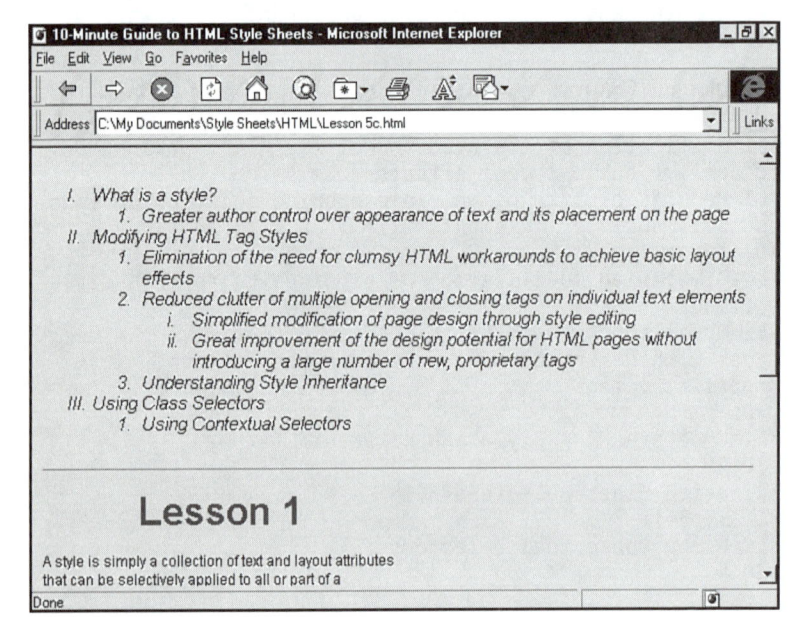

FIGURE 5.3 A single contextual selector can affect the appearance of an entire multi-level outline.

Be aware, however, that the ancestor specified in a contextual selector does not need to be an immediate parent. In the last example, an <LI> tag that is contained anywhere within <OL> tags satisfies the search and causes the style properties to be applied to it.

You are not limited to specifying only two generations in a contextual selector. If you modify the selector of the OL LI style from the last example to read OL OL LI, that style is applied to the second level `<LI>` elements in the outline (because they have two `<OL>` tags in their ancestry). However, the third level `<LI>` elements in the outline (and any deeper levels, if they existed) displays the same style properties because they share the same ancestry specified in the selector. To apply a different style to the third level elements, you must create a selector that identifies these elements uniquely, such as OL OL OL LI.

Modify the `<STYLE>` block of your **SAMPLE.HTML** files to appear as follows:

```
<STYLE>
<!--
H1      {font-size: 24pt;
    color: red;
    text-align: center}

H2      {font-size: 20pt;
    font-style: italic;
    color: blue}

BODY     {font-family: "Arial";
    background: yellow}

.left      {margin-right: 50%}

.right      {margin-left: 50%}

.center      {margin-left: 25%;
    margin-right: 25%}

OL LI        {font-size: 110%;
        font-weight: bold}

OL OL LI          {font-size: 100%;
        font-weight: medium}

OL OL OL LI      {font-style: italic;
        font-size: 90%;
        font-weight: medium}
-->
</STYLE>
```

Because the three contextual selectors at the end of the style block uniquely identify each of the outline's three levels, different style properties are applied to each, as shown in Figure 5.4.

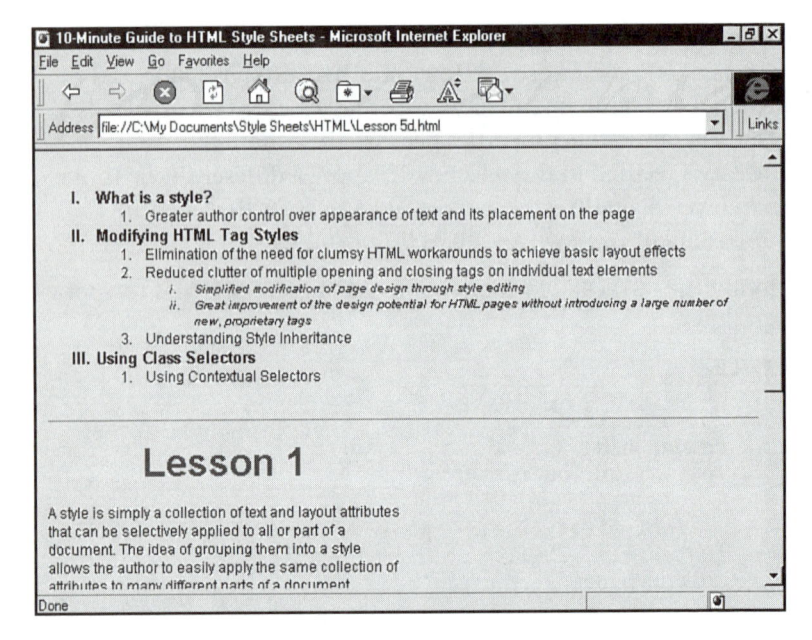

FIGURE 5.4   Contextual selectors can be used to identify specific elements deep inside a document's HTML hierarchy.

COMBINING SELECTORS

Contextual selectors can also be constructed using the class selectors described in Lesson 4. In the case of our **SAMPLE.HTML** file, a selector of OL LI.left would be perfectly valid and cause that style to be applied to any <LI CLASS=left> element contained within an <OL> element.

You can also use generic class selectors in a contextual format. A selector of OL.left would be equally valid and would stylize all elements contained within <OL> tags that have a left CLASS attribute.

In this lesson, you learned to apply styles to HTML elements based on their specific position within an HTML document. In the next lesson, you refine these skills by using new HTML tags to create discrete compartments within your documents in which to apply styles.

USING THE *<DIV>* AND *<SPAN>* TAGS

6

In this lesson, you learn several ways of applying styles with greater specificity using ID selectors and the <DIV> and <SPAN> tags.

As you learn about the use of class selectors and contextual selectors, it becomes clear that using HTML styles is primarily a matter of isolating specific text elements in your documents so that you can apply formatting properties to them. Styles provide an extensive array of properties that allow web page designers to control the appearance of text and manage the white space on the browser screen, but good designs come from juxtaposing elements on the canvas that have been formatted in different, but complementary ways.

USING THE *ID* SELECTOR

The different types of selectors covered in the previous lessons are very helpful in providing ways to isolate selected areas of a document, but sometimes they are still not precise enough. The ultimate in granularity of an HTML document is a case in which every element has its own individual style assigned to it through the use of a specialized selector that identifies it.

The CSS1 standard provides the means for just such a technique. The HTML 3 language specification includes an ID= attribute which is assigned a character string and inserted into a tag to uniquely identify it. Intended for use as a target by anchor references (as NAME= is currently used), it serves as a selector that identifies one specific tag in a document.

Attribute In HTML terms, an attribute is a parameter that can be added to a tag to alter or enhance its purpose. For example, the WIDTH= attribute can be added to the <HR> to specify the length of a horizontal rule, in the form <HR WIDTH=50%>.

To create a style for an ID selector, a unique character string is preceded by a number sign (#) and followed by a style declaration containing properties and values enclosed in curly braces in the usual manner. Thus, a typical ID selector would appear within an embedded <STYLE> block as follows:

```
#123abc          {font-size: 24pt; color: red}
```

The HTML element (to which the style is to be applied) is modified by the addition of the ID= attribute and the same character string. The properties last shown would be applied to an element appearing as follows:

```
<H1 ID=123abc>This is a Headline!</H1>
```

Any valid tag replaces the H1 and allows an ID selector to address any type of element, anywhere in a document.

While it has its uses in certain cases, the liberal application of ID selectors tends to defeat the overall purpose of HTML styles. The goal is to achieve the desired effect by creating the smallest possible number of style definitions and applying them to as many diverse elements as possible. Skillful use of the inheritance rules and careful definition of selectors saves keystrokes, eliminates code clutter, and helps you build a library of styles that can apply to all of the documents on your web site.

Using the *<DIV>* Tag

You may, at times, want to isolate a particular part of a document in order to apply styles within it. For example, you would like to modify the margins of some of the text blocks within <P> tags, while leaving other margins alone.

Adding class attributes or applying ID selectors is impractical on a large scale. The CSS1 standard, however, defines two new HTML elements that are used to isolate a portion of a document so that the application of styles is limited to only that portion.

<DIV> is one of the few new HTML tags introduced by the CSS1 standard. It is a means to create an artificial division in a document because the existing HTML architecture does not provide one. By enclosing elements within <DIV> and </DIV> tags, you can apply a default style to all of the enclosed elements or use DIV as part of contextual selectors to identify tags within the enclosure.

One of the biggest advantages of the <DIV> tag is that it has absolutely no effect on the appearance of a document except if it is used to assign styles. Browsers that do not support style sheets ignore the tag. It is preferable to use <DIV> rather than other HTML tags that might accomplish the same purpose (such as <TABLE>), because some may impose additional formatting attributes on the contents which may not be desired.

Modify your **SAMPLE.HTML** file by enclosing the last two paragraphs and headlines in the <BODY> block within <DIV> tags, as follows:

```
<HR>
<H1 CLASS=left>Lesson 1</H1>
<P CLASS=left> A style is simply a collection of text and
layout attributes that can be selectively applied to all
or part of a document. The idea of grouping them into a
style allows the author to easily apply the same
collection of attributes to many different parts of a
document.</P>
<DIV>
<H2 CLASS =right>The Default Browser Style</H2>
<P CLASS=right>HTML style sheets are innovative primarily
in that they allow various different styles to be applied
to web pages by the author. Indeed, it could be said that
all web browsers already use a style to display text.</p>
```

```
<H2 CLASS=center>The CSS1 Standard</H2>
<P CLASS=center>The HTML styles in Microsoft's Internet
Explorer 3.0 are based on a draft standard being
developed by the World Wide Web Consortium (W3C).</P>
</DIV>
</BODY>
```

If you reload the file in the browser at this time, you see that the
<DIV> tags do not change the appearance of the paragraphs. By
modifying the styles as shown, however, the application of the
class selectors is limited to the last two paragraphs of the document by placing them in the DIV context (see Figure 6.1).

```
<STYLE>
<!--
H1      {font-size: 24pt; color: red; text-align: center}

H2      {font-size: 20pt; font-style: italic; color: blue}

BODY     {font-family: "Arial"; background: yellow}

DIV .left        {margin-right: 50%}

DIV .right     {margin-left: 50%}

DIV .center     {margin-left: 25%; margin-right: 25%}

-->
</STYLE>
```

To further distinguish the contents of the <DIV> block, add the
following style definition, using DIV itself as the selector:

```
DIV     {font-family: "Times New Roman"; color: green}
```

You could, of course, achieve the same effect shown in Figure 6.2
by adding the font-family and color properties to the three styles
containing the .left, .right, and .center class selectors, but
why type the same properties three times when you only need to
do it once?

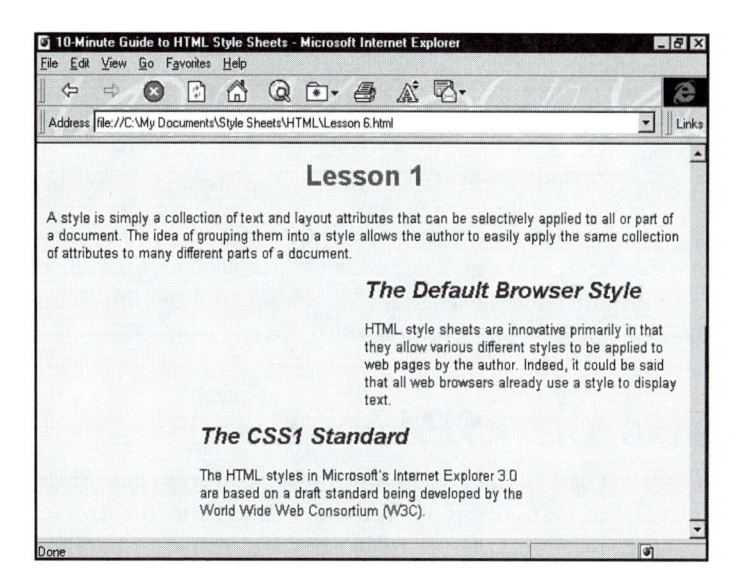

FIGURE 6.1   The <DIV> tags can be used to restrict the application of styles to a specific part of a document.

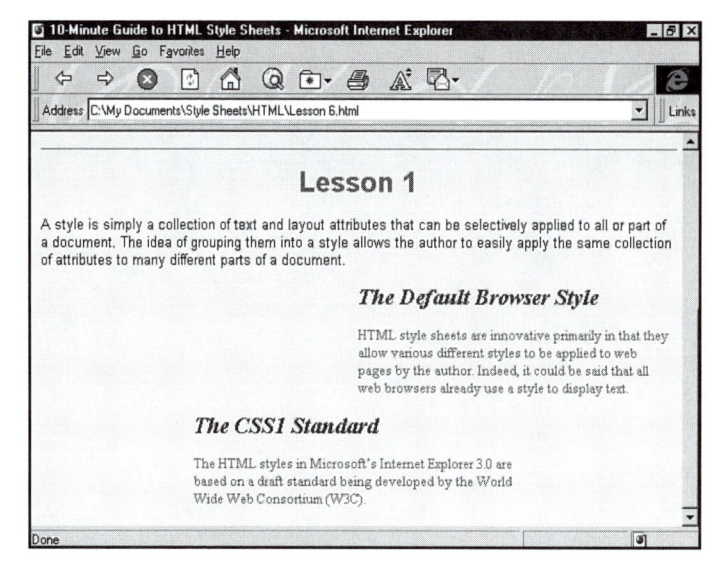

FIGURE 6.2   Styles can be applied to the <DIV> tag just like any other HTML element.

TIP

Inheritance in Practice Note that in the code used to create Figure 6.2, the color property has been used to make the paragraph text within the <DIV> tags green. However, the text of the headlines remains blue because whatever the order of the entries in the <STYLE> block, it is the ancestry of the HTML elements that controls inheritance. The <H2> tags are wholly contained within the <DIV> tags, making the blue of the H2 style the dominant color.

USING THE *<SPAN>* TAG

The <SPAN> tag is designed to perform the same function as the <DIV> tag, but without inserting the obligatory line break of a block element. Much as <EM> or <B> tags can be used to enclose a word, several words or even a single letter in order to alter its appearance, <SPAN> can be used within a block of text to apply styles to words or letters without having any effect in a browser that doesn't support styles.

If you add a style for the SPAN selector to **SAMPLE.HTML** as shown below, and then enclose selected letters or words in your <BODY> text with <SPAN> tags, you can create effects such as those shown in Figure 6.3.

```
SPAN     {font-size: 18pt}
```

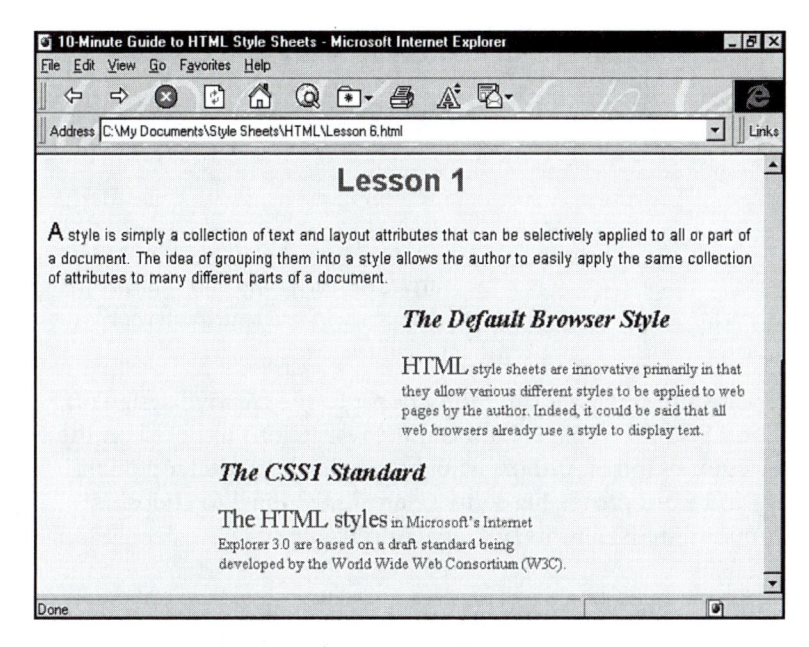

FIGURE 6.3   The <SPAN> tag is used to apply styles to small text selections without offsetting them from the rest of the element.

In this lesson, you learned to apply styles with extreme precision using ID selectors and the new HTML tags introduced in the CSS1 standard. In the next chapter, and those following, you learn the full capability of the formatting properties that you can include in your style definitions.

7

SPECIFYING
FONT FAMILIES

In this lesson, you learn about using styles to specify the font that the web browser will use to display your document's text.

Perhaps the single most limiting factor to the creative design of World Wide Web pages has been the restrictions imposed on the selection of fonts. Authors who are familiar with desktop publishing and word processing software are accustomed to choosing from hundreds of fonts of every conceivable style.

Font In the PC (and especially the Windows) community, the term *font* refers to the design of the letters used by a computer to display or print an alphabet. Referred to by names like Courier or Helvetica, these designs are actually typefaces. The term font refers to a particular typeface in a particular size and style, such as Univers 12pt Italic. However, the advent of scaleable font technologies like TrueType, which use one set of instructions to create type of any size, has resulted in the word *font* being used as a synonym of typeface.

Browsers are only capable of displaying text using the fonts installed on the reader's computer. Because the Windows operating systems ship with only a few basic fonts, authors must assume that a browser is able to display only Times New Roman, Arial, and Courier.

The problem is further compounded by the many platforms on which web browsers are run today. Even fonts that appear the same may be called by one name on a UNIX system and another on a Macintosh. The CSS1 standard provides style properties that allow authors to specify the exact fonts that are to be used when their documents are displayed. It also provides a means to account for different platforms, but this does not resolve the problem of users not owning the same fonts.

Printed Fonts versus Screen Fonts

The font capabilities of personal computers have traditionally been geared toward the production of printed output. Well designed digital fonts that produce superior printed text have traditionally brought premium prices, often up to $100 or more for a single typeface.

Displaying fonts online is an entirely different story, however. The skilled eyes of a printer or graphic designer can discern the subtle differences between good quality fonts and mediocre ones when text is printed at the 600 dpi (dots per inch) or greater resolution that is typically produced by laser printers.

The text on a computer monitor, however, typically displays at a resolution of well under 100 dpi, and the excellence of a top quality digital font is largely lost.

The font market has been glutted with low priced or even free typefaces in recent years that are rarely worth more than you pay for them. While these fonts may be unacceptable for high quality printed output, they will usually suffice for on-screen use.

As a result of these changes in the font market, there is no reason why digital fonts that are sufficient for web browser displays cannot be made freely available to all users. Microsoft has taken a large step in this direction by including a selection of fonts with the Internet Explorer 3.0 browser that complements those that are included with the Windows operating systems. These fonts are optimized for screen display, contain extensive international character sets, and are freely available for all users of the Windows and Macintosh operating systems.

Microsoft plans to make more fonts available in time, free for the downloading, but it is the incorporation of these new fonts into the browser's installation routine that is the primary reason why web page authors now assume the presence of these new fonts. The ability to display a document using the typefaces that the author intended, without the need for special preparations like downloading and installing new fonts, is what will make the World Wide Web into a fully functional environment for graphic designers.

THE WINDOWS/INTERNET EXPLORER FONTS

The combination of Windows 95 or Windows NT plus Microsoft Internet Explorer 3.0 furnish the computer with a minimum of the following six fonts, which are sure to be available to the web page designer (see Figure 7.1). Information on sample pages for these fonts can also be found in Appendix A:

- Arial
- Times New Roman
- Comic Sans MS
- Courier New
- Impact
- Verdana

TIP **Using Multiple Fonts** One of the most common failings of the novice desktop publisher is the tendency to use too many fonts in a single document. Now that the same font resources are being made available to web publishers, they are subject to the same danger. Avoid overloading your pages with different font families. Stick to one or two fonts and vary their appearance using sizes and weights instead.

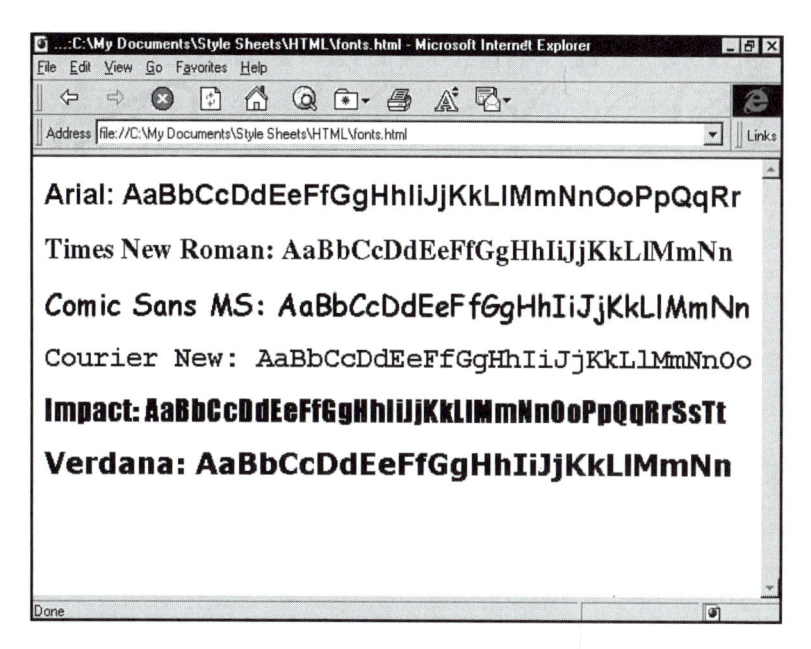

FIGURE 7.1   Windows and Internet Explorer provide web authors with a selection of six basic fonts that they can be certain their readers will have.

For any web page without styles, the default font that displays all text is the one set in the reader's browser. The default for both the Internet Explorer and the Netscape Navigator on the Windows platform is Times New Roman, which is one of the fonts that ships with the operating system. Readers can also customize their browsers to use any font that they have installed on their PCs as the default.

TIP

Browser Font Inheritance   Remember that the default browser font is inherited by every text element in an HTML page that does not have a `font-family` assigned to it with a style. This default font may, or may not, be Times New Roman, the original browser default. If you want your text displayed in Times New Roman, it is recommended that you create a style explicitly specifying it. Don't count on the browser default because the user may have changed it.

USING THE *FONT-FAMILY* PROPERTY

In order to specify the use of a particular font in a style, you must use the `font-family` property. The property is inserted between the curly braces that follow the font's selector; that is, the element to which the property is to be applied. As discussed in earlier lessons, the selector appears at the left margin on a new line and is followed by at least one space. The left curly bracket signals the beginning of the style *declaration* containing the style properties (and their accompanying values) that are to be applied to the selected text. Properties are separated from values by colons and semicolons separate each property:value combination.

 **Declaration** In HTML style sheets, a declaration is the entire series of properties and values enclosed by curly brackets. The declaration plus the selector is known as a *rule*.

A typical style rule specifying the use of a particular font appears as follows:

```
H1      {font-family: Arial}
```

If the name of the font family contains spaces, you must enclose the name in quotation marks, as shown:

```
H1      {font-family: "Times New Roman"}
```

Other properties can precede or follow the `font-family` property as long as each property:value combination is separated from the next by a semicolon. A rule containing multiple properties would appear as follows:

```
H1      {font-family: "Times New Roman";
        font-size: 14pt}
```

The `font-family` property controls only the basic font that displays the selected text. Other text formatting options, such as font size, weight, and style, are specified using separate properties.

Specifying Font Names   If you are specifying font-families other than those listed earlier, you must be sure to use the exact typeface name as it appears in Windows applications. To determine the typeface name, open the Fonts folder from the Windows Control Panel and double-click on the font you want to use. The typeface name appears on the second line of the font sample sheet that is displayed.

To experiment with the new fonts available to you, modify the <STYLE> block of your **SAMPLE.HTML** file to add the font-family property to your H1 and H2 selectors, as shown:

```
<STYLE>
<!--
H1      {font-family: Impact;
font-size: 24pt; color: red; text-align: center}

H2      {font-family: "Comic Sans MS";
font-size: 20pt; font-style: italic; color: blue}
```

Feel free to change the value of the font-family property for these and the other rules in your file. Good design comes from experimentation and styles are designed to provide you with the tools that you need.

SPECIFYING ALTERNATE FONTS

A web page author is not necessarily limited to using the six fonts shown in Figure 7.1. The name of any font installed on the author's computer can be specified in a style sheet. If that particular font is not installed on the reader's computer, the operating system substitutes the installed font that comes closest to having the same set of properties as the specified font.

In situations where a web page author has reason to believe that particular fonts are installed on readers' computers, there is nothing wrong with specifying other font families. If, for example, you are creating pages for an intranet web site (that is, a private site intended only for users of a corporate network), you can assemble a collection of licensed fonts and distribute them to your users or make sure that all company computers have those fonts pre-installed. This would also work if you were designing a web page intended for users of a particular software package that you know includes certain fonts.

Distributing Fonts While supplying fonts to your readers for installation on their machines may be a viable alternative on an intranet, don't consider this practice for Internet web pages unless you are absolutely certain that the fonts in question can be freely distributed without paying a license fee or obtaining permission. Fonts are software and their licensing practices have been a sore spot in the software industry for many years. Don't endanger yourself or your company by publicly violating font licensing agreements.

If you are unsure of the exact fonts installed on your readers' computers, or if your readers are using a mixture of Windows, Macintosh, and UNIX machines, you can specify alternative values for your `font-family` properties. Remember that some systems use different names for similar fonts. Simply list the alternative font names in the order that you want them to be selected, separating them with a comma and a space, as follows:

```
H1      {font-family: Arial, Helvetica, Helv}
```

Any `font-family` names that contain spaces must be enclosed in quotation marks. If you use a comma after a `font-family` name, it must be placed outside the trailing quote, contrary to standard English punctuation practices.

In this example, the browser attempts to display H1 text using the Arial font. If Arial is not present, the Helvetica (the Macintosh equivalent) will be substituted. If Helvetica is not present, then Helv (a variation on Helvetica and standard on many UNIX platforms) will be used.

Specifying Generic Font Types

Obviously, the technique of supplying alternative font names is to list the fonts in descending order of preference, hopefully ending with a font that you are certain everyone has. When you are dealing with multiple platforms, this is not always easy. The CSS1 standard, therefore, defines a number of generic font-family names that can be included in your alternative list as a last resort.

Generic font-family names can be added to any alternative font-family list, just as if they were normal font names. They are typically added last, so that they are used when no other matching font name is found.

The generic font types defined by the CSS1 standard are as follows:

- Serif
- Sans serif
- Cursive
- Fantasy
- Monospace

These are all traditional typographical terms used to describe general font styles. A serif font is one, like Times New Roman, in which the letters have small decorative ends, such as those that descend from the ends of the crossbar on the letter T (see Figure 7.2). These decorative ends are themselves called *serifs*, and a sans serif font (in French, sans means without) is one that does not have these decorations, such as Arial.

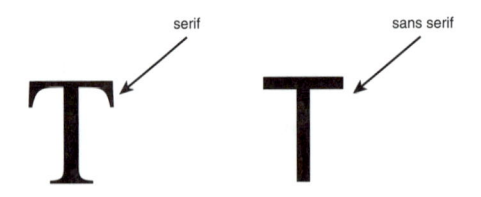

FIGURE 7.2   The two most basic types of fonts are serif and sans serif, which are distinguished by the presence (or absence) of decorative ends on the letters.

A cursive font is one that resembles a calligraphic longhand with separated letters, and fantasy indicates a more decorative type of font, more likely to be used for headlines than body text. A monospaced font, like Courier New, is one in which each letter of the alphabet is exactly the same width. The browser's default monospaced font has always been available to web page authors through the use of the `<PRE>` and `<TT>` tags. Monospaced fonts are often used for directory listings and to present text in columns (so that a consistent number of spaces will always result in even columns).

Therefore, to cover all possibilities, you are likely to end up with `font-family` properties that look something like the following, which provides the desired font, a standard Macintosh alternative, a possible UNIX alternative, and finally a generic family that can be interpreted by a browser on any platform:

```
H1      {font-family: Arial, Helvetica, Helv, sans-serif}
```

In this lesson, you learned how to specify the font that is to be used to display the text in your web pages. In the next lesson, you learn how to vary the size of your text.

SPECIFYING FONT SIZE

In this lesson, you learn how to create styles that specify the size of the text on your web pages.

Using blocks of different sized text is one of the most fundamental web page design techniques, and it is usually one of the first skills learned by students of the HTML language. The basic HTML tags provide for variations in font size primarily in the form of paragraph text and six boldface headline tags, ranging from largest to smallest, and numbered from H1 to H6, as shown in Figure 8.1.

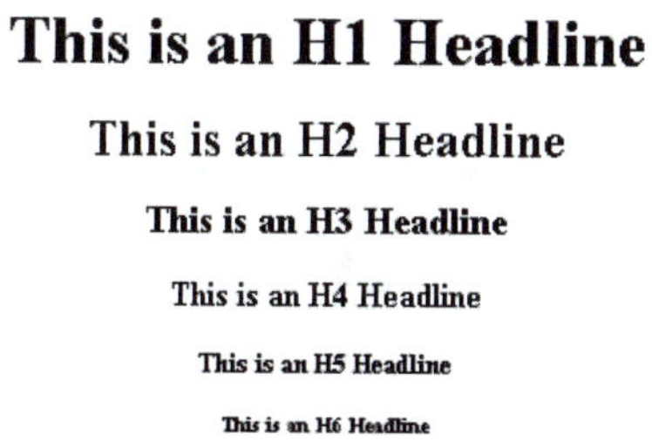

This is an H1 Headline

This is an H2 Headline

This is an H3 Headline

This is an H4 Headline

This is an H5 Headline

This is an H6 Headline

FIGURE 8.1 Standard HTML coding can produce headline text in only six sizes.

A Netscape revision to the HTML language added a `<FONT>` tag which provides web page designers with more control. It allows the font size to be specified without the bold style imposed by the headline tags, but it is still limited in its flexibility. It cannot create text that falls between the default sizes.

This, ironically, is a throwback to the way that digital fonts used to be. At one time, a typeface was sold as a collection of bitmaps with each size requiring a different file. At that time, a particular typeface in a particular size, such as 12-point Helvetica, was considered to be a font. You would purchase a typeface package and receive a collection of fonts in different sizes that you would download to your printer and command your application to use.

Then scaleable font technologies came along, like Adobe Type Manager and TrueType, that use a single set of font instructions for each typeface to create text of almost any size. The ability to scale fonts in applications and in printers revolutionized the desktop publishing industry, and the CSS1 standard is designed to provide the same service to web publishers.

USING THE *FONT-SIZE* PROPERTY

With the `font-size` property in a style declaration, you can specify font sizes for your text with almost the same precision as a word processor or page layout program. Sizes can be specified in several different ways, using absolute or relative measurements, and very fine adjustments (down to 1 point, or 1/72 inch) can be applied, as shown in Figure 8.2.

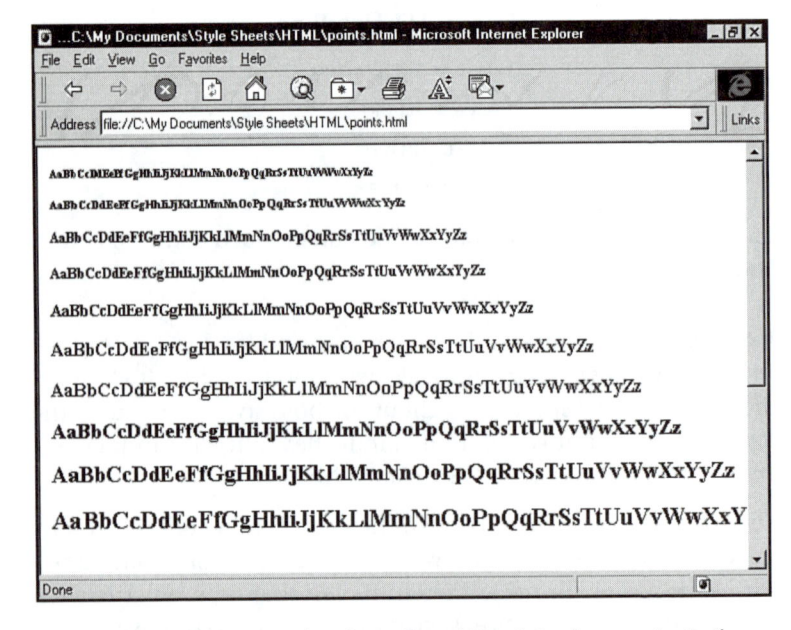

FIGURE 8.2   Font samples from 7 to 16 points demonstrate the precise control over font sizes provided by HTML styles.

The syntax for specifying font sizes in a style is the same as that for most of the properties in the CSS1 standard. The `font-size` property name follows the selector, followed by a value that is specified as an absolute measurement, a relative keyword, or a relative measurement. A typical style rule controlling font size would appear as follows:

```
P     {font-size: 14pt}
```

USING ABSOLUTE FONT SIZES

You can express absolute font size values by using the following measurements (shown with their accepted abbreviations in parentheses):

- Points (`pt`)
- Pixels (`px`)
- Centimeters (`cm`)
- Inches (`in`)
- Ems (`em`)

Absolute Value   An absolute value is one that is not reliant on any other value. Text that has been assigned an absolute font size will always be identical in size to any other text with the same assigned value in that environment.

Point   The point is a traditional unit of type size measurement that dates back before the time of digital typesetting. One point equals approximately 1/72 or 0.01383 inches.

 **Em** For the `font-size` property, an em is a unit of length corresponding to the font size of the parent element. Measurements supplied in ems are therefore scaleable to screen displays of different resolutions. Internet Explorer 3.0 does not support the use of measurements in ems.

The scales used to measure absolute `font-size` values can be mixed within a document, and decimal values can be used to specify fractions of units. Absolute values are expressed by listing the numerical value immediately followed by the abbreviation for the unit of measurement, as in the following examples:

```
H1      {font-size: .75in}
H2      {font-size: 24pt}
H3      {font-size: .5cm}
H4      {font-size: 10px}
```

It must be understood that while these size measurements are referred to as absolute values, they are, in fact, relative to the size and resolution of the monitor on which they are displayed. If you specify a font size of one inch, and then measure the image that displays on your monitor, it will very likely not be anywhere near an exact inch. Software is usually designed for linear accuracy in the printing of fonts, rather than their screen display.

The measurements that display on your monitor, however, will be consistent. The one inch font will be equal in size (on your monitor) to a 72-point font, or to a 2.54 centimeter font. Pixels cannot be equated in this way, because the size of a single pixel varies, depending on your screen resolution and the size of your monitor.

Using *size* Keywords

There are font size keywords supported by the CSS1 standard, that also have absolute values, but their values are dependent on settings imposed by the browser. In addition to using absolute values that are numerical, you can also use any of the following terms:

- xx-large

- x-large

- large

- medium

- small

- x-small

- xx-small

The style syntax is the same, with the keyword simply replacing the numerical measurement, as follows:

```
H1      {font-size: x-large}
```

The relationship between these sizes is equivalent to that of the H1 through H6 headline tags, leaving them subject to the same limitations as headlines. The CSS1 standard recommends a 1.5:1 size ratio for the keyword values, meaning that large text should be 1 1/2 times the size of medium text. However, this ratio, as well as the base font size on which the ratios are calculated, is controlled by the browser and usually cannot be adjusted by the user.

Relative Font Sizes

Font-size is an inherited property, meaning that a font size value that is applied to a particular HTML element is passed down to all of the other elements contained within it. As a result of this relationship, you can also specify font sizes in relative terms, based on the size of the element's immediate parent.

If, for example, you create a style for the <BODY> tag that includes the font-size property and a value of 14 points, you can then apply the font-size property to the H1 tag (which will be contained within the <BODY> tags) using a value that is relative to the 14-point body text size.

Relative font sizes can be expressed in three ways:

- Relative keywords (larger/smaller)
- Numerical relatives (+2, –1, and so on)
- Percentages

Keyword and numerical relatives are based on the keyword sizes discussed in the "Using `size` Keywords" section, earlier in this lesson. A `font-size` value of `larger` will cause the font to be enlarged from the parent element's size to the next higher keyword value. Thus, if the `<BODY>` tag is assigned a `font-size` value of `medium`, large text will be displayed when the `<H2>` tag is assigned a `font-size` value of `larger`.

Numerical relatives can be used when you wish to enlarge or reduce text size by two or more keyword units. Numerical relatives are used by the `font-size` property by default if you specify a numerical value without a unit of measurement (such as inches or points). A `font-size` value of +2 will cause medium sized text to be enlarged to `x-large` (jumping two units), while a –2 value will reduce it to `x-small`.

Finally, relative values can be expressed as percentages, which are typically used in relation to an absolute numerical measurement. A `font-size` value of `200%` causes text to be displayed at twice the size of the text in the parent element. Obviously, using percentages provides much greater flexibility, as you are not bound to the browser's six standard font sizes.

Following are examples of each of the relative `font-size` values:

```
H2      {font-size: larger}
H2      {font-size: +1}
H2      {font-size: 150%}
```

Assuming that a browser uses the 1.5:1 ratio recommended by the CSS1 standard, the three declarations shown will all result in the same font size.

Explorer Support   Internet Explorer 3.0 does not support the numerical and keyword relative values for the `font-size` property as defined in the CSS1 standard at this time. Support for relative `font-size` values using percentages is supported.

The use of relative values in an HTML document with several generations can become extremely complicated. Remember that a relative value for a property is always computed based on the parent element's actual value for that property.

Thus, in the following example, if the <BODY> tag is assigned an absolute `font-size` value of 16 points, and the <H1> tag is defined as 200%, the <H1> text will be twice as large as the <BODY> text, or 32 points. If the <SPAN> tag is also defined as having a 200% `font-size`, its text calculates at 200% of the <H1> text's actual size, causing the <SPAN> text to be 64 points in size.

```
<BODY>
<H1><SPAN>T</SPAN>his is a Headline</H1>
</BODY>
```

To familiarize yourself with the various ways of specifying font sizes, add a `font-size` property to the BODY selector in the <STYLE> block of your **SAMPLE.HTML** file (shown later). You can experiment with the different scales of measurement by modifying the sizes of the H1, H2, and BODY tags.

To see the effect of relative font sizes, modify the percentages applied to the OL LI, OL OL LI, and OL OL OL LI selectors to format the elements of the ordered list you created in Lesson 5.

You can also try adding the `font-size` property to other declarations, such as those for the .left, .right, and .center class selectors, and see the effects of your changes.

```
<STYLE>
<!--
H1      {font-family: "Impact";
font-size: 24pt;
     color: red;
     text-align: center}

H2      {font-family: "Comic Sans MS";
font-size: 20pt;
     font-style: italic;
     color: blue}

BODY    {font-size: 14pt;
font-family: "Arial";
     background: yellow}

.left   {margin-right: 50%}

.right    {margin-left: 50%}

.center    {margin-left: 25%;
     margin-right: 25%}

OL LI        {font-size: 110%;
          font-weight: bold}

OL OL LI        {font-size: 100%;
          font-weight: medium}

OL OL OL LI    {font-style: italic;
          font-size: 90%;
          font-weight: medium}
-->
</STYLE>
```

 **TIP** **Font Size Units** Although mixing different size units, such as points, inches, and centimeters, is useful as an exercise, it is best to avoid confusion by selecting a single method of assigning font sizes and sticking to it. The same results can be achieved with any of the measurement scales, so the choice is strictly one of personal preference.

In this lesson, you learned the different means of specifying font sizes in HTML styles. In the next lesson, you learn how to modify a font's appearance by changing its weight.

MODIFYING TEXT ATTRIBUTES— PART I

In this lesson and the next one, you learn to control the application of text attributes like boldface, italics, and underlining with styles.

Apart from the selection of a font family and a font size, there are several other attributes that you can apply to your text to emphasize certain passages or to contrast one block of text from another. These attributes should be familiar to users of word processing or desktop publishing software.

The CSS1 standard separates these text attributes into four different properties and are listed with their primary purpose:

- font-weight—Boldfaces text

- font-style—Italicizes text

- text-decoration—Underlines text

- text-transform—Modifies the case of selected text

This division of the attributes into different properties allows you to easily assign more than one to a single selector, and makes it possible to combine the attributes. It also allows you to control the removal of these attributes when they are inherited from parent elements without the need for the duplication of complex properties.

It still may seem odd that each of the properties listed has only one option, when the font-family and font-size properties, for example, have so many. This is because the listing shows only the options that are supported in the 3.0 version of Microsoft's Internet Explorer. The CSS1 standard includes many useful font control features in these properties that are not yet supported by the Internet Explorer for a variety of reasons. The CSS1 standard is still undergoing development.

It is hoped that future versions of the browser (and of the other browsers promising support for style sheets) will allow the additional values for these properties to be used, as defined by the standard. With that in mind, these lessons will cover the unsupported options (while notating them), in order to show the potential value of HTML style sheets to web publishers.

Using the *font-weight* Property

The `font-weight` property controls the thickness of the lines that make up an alphabet. Anyone who has worked with HTML has used the `<B>` or `<STRONG>` tag to create boldface type. Styles allow you to combine the `font-weight` with other properties in a single style declaration to achieve an overall effect with a single tag that would require several different tags, using traditional HTML coding.

Font weights are defined in style declarations by specifying a keyword as the value for the `font-weight` property, as shown:

```
P       {font-weight: bold}
```

The default weight is medium, which can be assigned to a child element to return it to its normal weight when a different value is inherited from a parent element. For example, to prevent a headline tag from using bold type, you would create a rule like this:

```
H1      {font-weight: medium}
```

Absolute Weights

The CSS1 standard defines seven possible absolute values for the `font-weight` property:

- `extra-light`
- `light`
- `demi-light`
- `medium`

- `demi-bold`

- `bold`

- `extra-bold`

 **Explorer Support**   Internet Explorer 3.0 supports only the medium and bold values for the `font-weight` property. Any other specified value will be ignored.

The ideal situation for the use of these values would be a font that provides separate typestyle variants for all of the different weights shown. As with italics, a true font variant created by a designer is preferable to one that is approximated by software interpolation. However, few fonts are available in all of these weights. Of the six fonts included with the Internet Explorer, all have bold variants except for Impact, and none have variants for any other weights.

Future browser releases will no doubt offer support for more of the weights specified in the CSS1 standard, through interpolation if actual variants are not available. The results, as with boldface and italics, are always highly dependant on the individual font being modified.

 **Typestyle Variants**   Fonts often include alternate alphabets in various typestyles. Typically, a font family consists of a medium weight, a bold, an italic, and a bold italic. Other (usually more expensive) font packages may include various other weights in combination with italics, small caps, condensed type, or other special effects. You can see what variants are included with your fonts by looking in the Fonts Control Panel in Windows, where each of the variants is listed separately.

When a font includes a bold variant, specifying the bold value for the `font-weight` property causes the variant to be used. When a font does not include a bold variant, the browser approximates one by increasing the thickness of every letter in the alphabet by a uniform amount. Depending on the font and its size, the results of this technique may range from acceptable to miserable.

In Figure 9.1, if you look carefully, you can see the differences between the Times New Roman medium and bold faces, particularly in the lowercase letters e, o, and h, indicating that they have been individually designed for readability at their respective weights. The Impact boldface text doesn't look nearly as good as the medium weight because the font does not include a bold variant. Each line has been fattened by the same amount everywhere, to the point at which the counters (the enclosed or hollow parts of the letters) look as though they are about to close up completely.

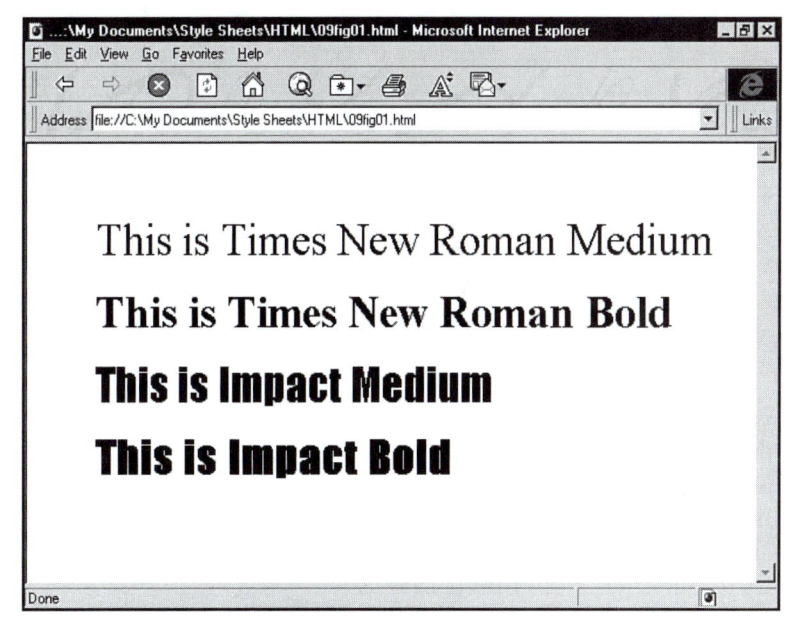

FIGURE 9.1 Fonts that include variants for different typestyles are always preferable to software approximations.

> **Specifying Variants**   Internet Explorer 3.0 may be incapable of simulating all the various weights indicated by the `font-weight` keywords, but if you are using a font that includes variants with their own names, you can use them in your web pages by specifying the full name of the variant as a value for the `font-family` property. For example, a `font-family` value of Helvetica Light causes the font of that name to be used, regardless of its weight. Be sure to specify the exact typeface name for the variant as it appears in a Windows application's font selector.

To experiment with font weights, you can make changes in your **SAMPLE.HTML** file that modify the weights already defined in the styles for the ordered list you created in Lesson 5, as shown.

```
OL LI           {font-size: 110%;
          font-weight: bold}


OL OL LI            {font-size: 100%;
          font-weight: medium}


OL OL OL LI     {font-style: italic;
          font-size: 90%;
          font-weight: medium}
```

`font-weight` is an inherited property, so you must be conscious of your document's HTML structure when you apply it. As with all of the text attributes that you can apply with styles, turning them off can be as important as turning them on. In the example just shown, the specification of the medium weight for the `OL OL LI` and `OL OL OL LI` selectors is necessary to override the bold value that is inherited from the `OL LI` selector.

RELATIVE WEIGHTS

The CSS1 standard also defines two relative values for the `font-weight` property:

- `bolder`
- `lighter`

The bolder and lighter values modify the weights relative to the absolute value keywords listed earlier. `font-weight` is different from other properties because specifying a relative value causes the inherited weight to be increased or decreased by two units, not one. Therefore, application of the bolder value would cause an element inheriting a medium `font-weight` to skip the demi-bold weight and display as bold.

As always, the relative value is applied to the actual value of the parent element. In the next example, if the <BODY> tag is assigned a medium weight, and the <H1> tag is defined as bolder, a value of lighter applied to the <SPAN> tag would return the text to medium weight, as <SPAN> is the child element of <H1>.

```
<BODY>
<H1><SPAN>T</SPAN>his is a headline.</H1>
</BODY>
```

 **Explorer Support**   Because Internet Explorer 3.0 can only display two adjacent font weights, medium and bold, the relative values are not supported.

In this lesson, you learned how to modify the weight of selected text. In the next lesson, you modify other text attributes, such as italics and underlines.

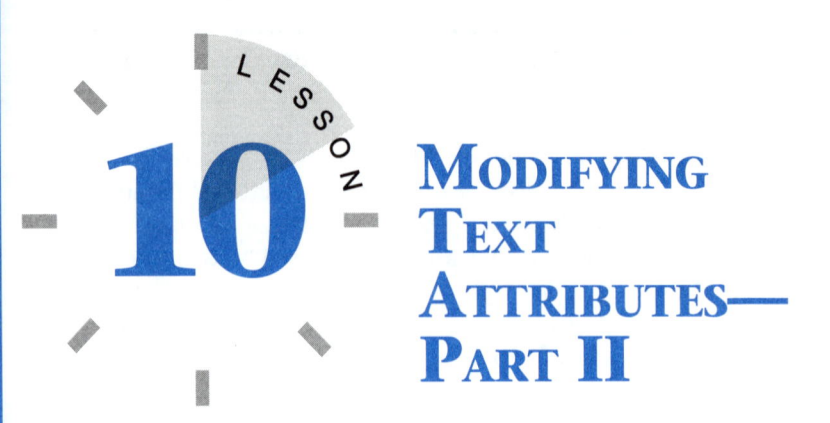

LESSON 10

MODIFYING TEXT ATTRIBUTES— PART II

In this lesson, you learn other ways to modify the appearance of the text in your web pages.

The last lesson covered the first of the text attribute properties defined by the CSS1 standard: `font-weight`. This lesson covers the other three that provide many ways to make your documents more attractive and readable.

Unfortunately, as stated in Lesson 9, some of the text attribute functions defined in the style sheet standard are not yet supported by the Internet Explorer 3.0 browser.

USING THE *FONT-STYLE* PROPERTY

The `font-style` property allows you to specify the use of different typestyles that alter the appearance of your fonts. Unlike `font-weight`, this property is not quantitative. Its values function as toggles that turn the desired effect on and off as needed.

The CSS1 standard defines four values for use with the `font-style` property:

- `normal`
- `italic`
- `oblique`
- `small caps`

An oblique font is, in appearance, synonymous with an italic. Some font families use the word oblique for their slanted variants, but most use italic. The CSS1 standard calls for the substitution of an oblique when an italic is not found. As with the bold `font-weight`, an italic font will be approximated by the browser if neither an italic or an oblique variant is found. (See Lesson 9 for a discussion of font approximation.)

The italic fonts simulated by a software application are worse than the boldface ones and should be avoided, if possible. In Figure 10.1, you can easily see that a true italic, like that of Times New Roman, is a completely different design, whereas the simulated Impact italic is simply slanted to the right.

Of the six fonts native to Internet Explorer 3.0, all but Impact and Comic Sans MS have Italic and Bold Italic variants.

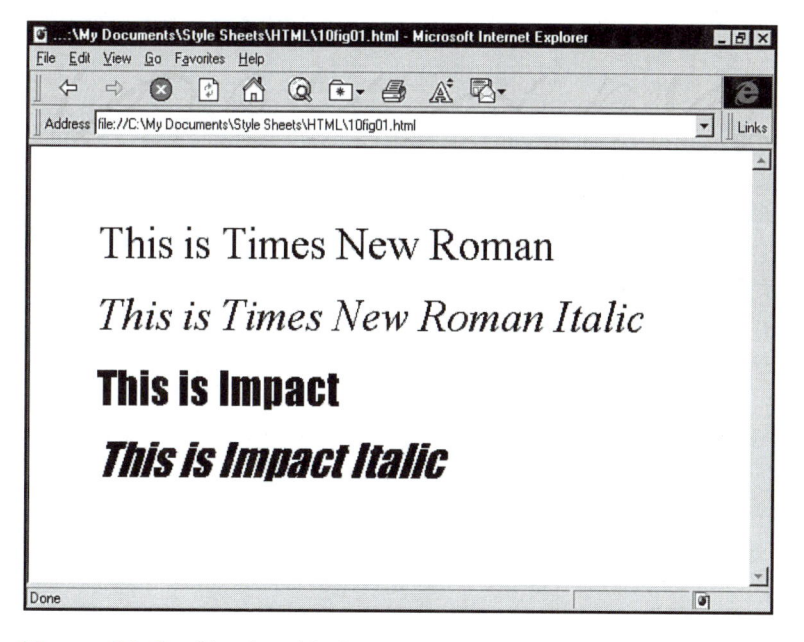

FIGURE 10.1 Simulated italics simply slant the existing font, whereas a true italic has a different, almost calligraphic style.

Small caps refers to an alternative alphabet that uses characters that are uppercase in design but lowercase in size, as shown in Figure 10.2. They are typically used in situations where full-sized caps would be inappropriately large, such as when mixed with normal text.

The standard allows for a browser to substitute an uppercase alphabet at a smaller size for a true small caps variant, which is rare, especially in TrueType fonts. A software interpolation of this type often is acceptable because no change is being made to the appearance of the font. In some cases, however, simulated small caps can appear too light when mixed with text using the same typeface at normal size.

THE QUICK BROWN FOX
JUMPS OVER THE LAZY DOG

FIGURE 10.2 Small caps are effectively used in places where uppercase text would be intrusive.

You can assign multiple values to the font-style property that activate two options for the same block of text. The small-caps value can be combined with either italic or oblique. Multiple values can be specified in any order, with only a space between them, as shown in the first rule below:

```
H1          {font-style: italic small-caps}
H1 SPAN        {font-style: italic}
```

Explorer Support Internet Explorer 3.0 only supports the normal and italic values for the font-style property. It ignores any other specified values.

Please note that when the font-style property is inherited, the entire property is passed down from the parent element to the child, but not the individual values. If a parent element is assigned both the `italic` and the `small-caps` values, as shown in the example for the `H1` selector, the text within the `<SPAN>` tags only displays in italics. The entire property is overridden by the declaration assigned to the `H1 SPAN` selector, and the `small-caps` value is not inherited.

USING THE *TEXT-DECORATION* PROPERTY

The `text-decoration` property allows you to apply certain special effects to a font. As with the `font-style` property, the values are toggles and can only be turned on or off.

The effects include:

- `none`
- `underline`
- `overline`
- `line-through`
- `blink`

 **Explorer Support** Internet Explorer 3.0 only supports the `underline` and `line-through` values for the `text-decoration` property. It ignores any other specified values.

The effects applied by the `text-decoration` property (unlike those of the `font-weight` and `font-style` properties) are always created in the browser and can be applied to any font without concern for the existence of typestyle variants. Because of this, the appearance of text with these attributes can vary widely. Some fonts, especially decorative ones like cursives and scripts, may look absurd when underlined. If you are using fonts other than those that are native to Internet Explorer 3.0, be sure to view the results of your efforts carefully.

text-decoration values are not inherited in the same way as those of other properties. If a parent element is underlined, the child elements enclosed within it will be underlined as well. If, however, the line-through value is then applied to one of the child elements, the inherited property will not be overridden. The resulting text will have an underline as well as a line-through.

You can achieve this same effect by applying the same property to a single selector twice, with different values. For example, the appearance of <P> text in the Internet Explorer using the following rules:

```
BODY     {text-decoration: underline}
P        {text-decoration: line-through}
```

would be the same as when using this rule:

```
P        {text-decoration: underline;
          text-decoration: line-through}
```

The only way to remove a parent element's text-decoration value from a child element is to explicitly apply the none value to the child.

This is an odd situation that appears to be the result of a somewhat ambiguous passage in the CSS1 standard. Because the underline value is likely to be the only one employed by most users of the text-decoration property, no great problems should result.

Using the *Text-Transform* Property

The text-transform property, which is not yet supported by Internet Explorer 3.0, allows the use of styles to modify the case of selected text. This can be a useful tool for web designers who must deal with imported text using tools that lack a case changing function.

Accepted values are as follows:

- `none`
- `capitalize`
- `uppercase`
- `lowercase`

The `capitalize` value changes the first letter of each word in the selected text block to uppercase. The `uppercase` and `lowercase` values change the case of the entire word. The values are notated as in the following example:

```
H1        {text-transform: uppercase}
```

`text-transform` is an inherited property, and it is easy to see how this could lead to problems in complex HTML documents. Applying a value to an HTML tag that has many child elements could require more effort to reset the property to `none` in all the right places than simply retyping the text.

In this lesson, you learned how to apply special attributes to alter the appearance of your text. In the next lesson, you learn how to use margin properties to precisely place text elements on your web pages.

11

SPECIFYING MARGIN VALUES

In this lesson, you learn to place text elements on your web pages using margins.

A serious shortcoming of HTML is the difficulty of locating objects on web pages. The acceptance of tables has mitigated this somewhat. Tables make it possible to align text down the right side of the page. Style sheets provide web page authors with a whole new page layout facility, in the form of margins.

On a web page using styles, every block element can have a margin around all four of its sides, which are individually adjustable using absolute or relative values. Margins allow text blocks of any size to be created and placed anywhere on the canvas.

 **Block Element**   A block element is any HTML element that is automatically offset from its adjacent elements by a line space. For example, the <P> and <H1> tags are block elements, but the <EM> and <I> tags are not.

PAGE LAYOUT TECHNIQUES WITH STYLES

Along with font control, margins are the most crucial elements of the CSS1 standard because they bring the field of web page design almost to the level of desktop publishing. Unfortunately, this is an area in which Internet Explorer's support for the standard is incomplete.

Margins allow you to locate text blocks of any size at precise locations on the canvas. You can modify the weight, color, and pattern of the border line surrounding the text, or just make it transparent. By bringing web page design closer to the long-standing principles of the printed page, the entire web publishing paradigm can be simplified through the use of pre-existing skills, tools, and techniques.

The standard defines every block element in a document as having padding, a border, and a margin around all four sides, in that order. The *padding* is the area of space between the contents of the text block and the margin. The *border* is a rectangular line surrounding the padding and the enclosed contents. The *margin* surrounds the border, completing the pattern of three adjustable barriers, as shown in Figure 11.1.

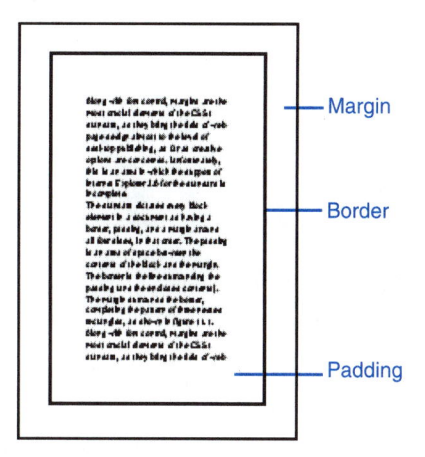

FIGURE 11.1 The CSS1 standard provides for three adjustable barriers surrounding every block element in an HTML document.

All three of these elements can be adjusted using styles. The bor-der property can be applied to specify the thickness of the line. It can also be assigned a color or a graphic image as a fill. The pad-ding property lets you adjust the size of the space between the border and the contents with absolute or relative measurements.

Internet Explorer 3.0 does not support the `border` and `padding` properties but does support the `margin` properties. The `margin` properties provide enough flexibility to demonstrate how much potential there is in the concept of page layout with styles.

Using the *margin* Properties

There are four individual margin properties defined in the CSS1 standard—one for each side of a block element. They are named as follows:

- `margin-left`
- `margin-right`
- `margin-top`
- `margin-bottom`

Explorer Support   Internet Explorer 3.0 does not support the `margin-bottom` property as defined in the CSS1 standard. In addition, the `margin-top` property, added to the final version of the browser just before its release, does not function properly, and creates margins far larger than their measurements.

Margin values are not inherited, in the strict sense of the word, but they are cumulative. The value for each `margin` property represents the distance from the margin of its adjacent element. That is, if a document's `<BODY>` tag has been set to use a 1-inch margin on the left side, a block of text enclosed by `<P>` tags with the same 1-inch margin setting will begin at a point 2 inches from the edge of the page.

The exception to this rule occurs when two elements with opposing margins are stacked vertically. If an element with a `margin-bottom` value is directly atop an element with a `margin-top` value, the margins should *collapse*, and only the larger of the two values is applied.

 **Explorer Support** The inheritance of margin properties is the area where the implementation of style sheets in Internet Explorer 3.0 differs most drastically from the CSS1 standard. In many cases, the value of a left or right margin in a child element replaces and overrides that of a parent, when the standard explicitly says that it shouldn't. This behavior, however, is not consistent. At this time, trail and error is an essential part of working with margin settings. Internet Explorer 3.01 treats the left and right margins properly, but until you can be certain that your readers are using an updated browser, I recommend that you don't create permanent style sheets for large-scale document conversions.

By default, margins are transparent, so the color or graphic pattern used by the parent element is still visible under the margin of a child element (unless the background property is applied with a different value).

Absolute Measurements

Margin properties are notated much like other style properties, with a value specified after the property name, and separated by a colon and a space. Measurements can be specified using any one of the scales supported by the CSS1 standard, including:

- Points (pt)
- Inches (in)
- Centimeters (cm)
- Pixels (px)
- Ems (em)

 Explorer Support Internet Explorer 3.0 provides no support for em measurements in any of its properties but relative measurements can be supplied using percentages.

Typical margin properties would appear in a style sheet as follows:

```
BODY            {margin-left: 1in;
            margin-right: 2.54cm;
margin-top: 72pt}
```

As with all of the absolute measurements used in style sheets, you must account for the differences in monitor size and screen resolution. A 1-inch margin setting will not appear on every screen as exactly one inch, and documents styled with absolute margins can look very different on computers running at different resolutions.

When a web page with margins displays in the Internet Explorer, the screen is divided into three parts: the left margin, the content, and the right margin. If the margins are assigned absolute sizes, the width of the content area varies according to the size and resolution of the display. If the content is text, this could mean that a browser displayed at 640×480 pixels will have 5 words per line of text, while the same document could have up to 10 words per line at 1024×768 pixels.

For a page design such as Figure 11.2, absolute measurements may be acceptable. This document uses margins in a very simple way—to emphasize the headline by offsetting it to the left of a centered paragraph. The paragraph text adjusts itself to different screen resolutions, but the effect is still readable.

There may be other times when you have a number of different elements on the page and you want to keep the relationships between them absolutely consistent. You will then have to use relative measurements to specify your margin properties.

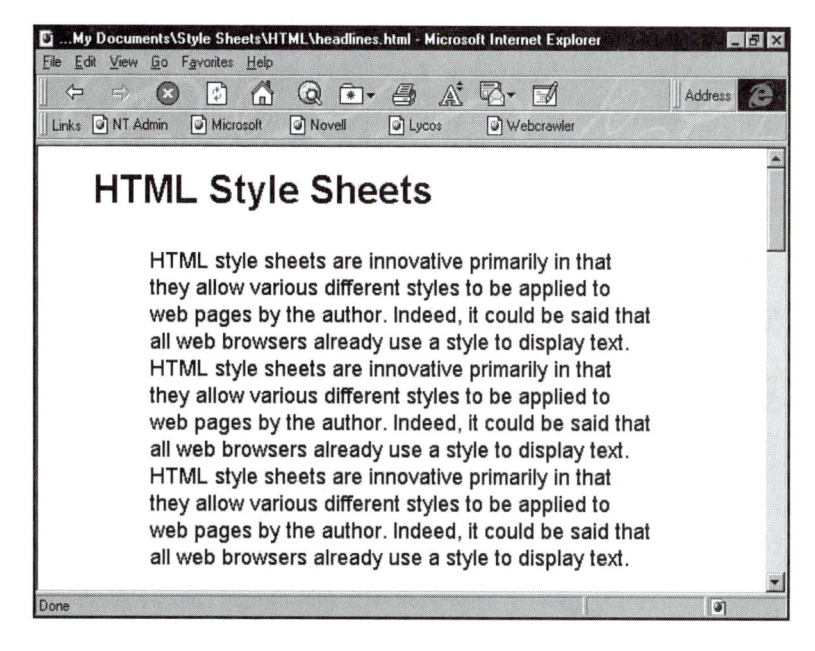

Figure 11.2 Margin values specified with absolute measurements are useful in documents that are consistently formatted and relatively plain.

Relative Measurements

Relative measurements for margin properties are specified using percentages that are measured against the parent element's size from border to border. When you want to place an element in a specific area of the browser screen, relative measurements ensure that the element always appears in the same place in relation to the other screen elements.

As an example, recall the paragraphs that you used to practice creating class selectors in Lesson 4. You created three generic class selectors in your **SAMPLE.HTML** file that appear as follows:

```
.left      {margin-right: 50%}
.right     {margin-left: 50%}
.center    {margin-left: 25%; margin-right: 25%}
```

Each of these classes specifies a total of 50% margin space, isolating exactly half of the browser screen's width for the display of text. Varying the percentages from margin-left to margin-right allows the three blocks of text in Figure 4.2 to be scattered around the screen in a consistent pattern. You may be able to use absolute measurements to achieve the same effect on your monitor, but when viewing the document on other systems, you could end up with text blocks of varying widths and erratic placement of your elements.

USING NEGATIVE MARGIN VALUES

You can also create interesting effects with `margin` properties by assigning negative values to them. In this way, you can force a text element to be extended outside of its block, superimposing it over a graphic or another text block, as shown in Figure 11.3.

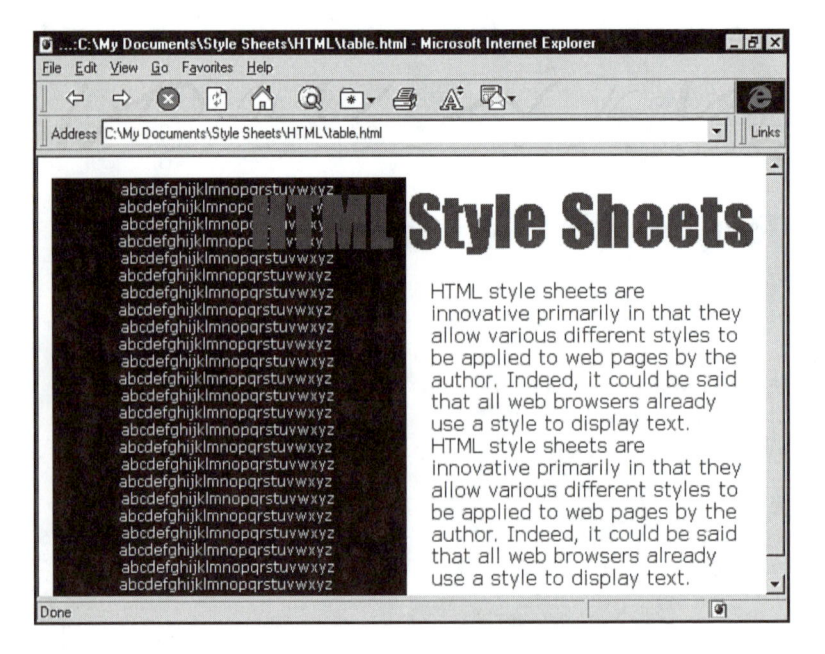

FIGURE 11.3 By assigning a negative value to a margin property, text on a web page can be superimposed over other text.

The HTML code used to create the figure is as follows:

```
<HTML>
<HEAD>
<STYLE>
<!--
H1      {font-size: 56;
         color: red;
         text-align: right;
         margin-left: -75%;
         font-family: Impact}

P       {font-family: Verdana}

.right  {color: blue;
         margin-left: 16pt}

.left   {font-size: 12;
         color: white}
-->
</STYLE>
</HEAD>
<BODY BGCOLOR=white>
<TABLE>
<TD WIDTH=50% ALIGN=center VALIGN=TOP
    STYLE="background: black">
<P CLASS=left>
abcdefghijklmnopqrstuvwxyz<br>abcdefghijklmnopqrstuvwxyz
abcdefghijklmnopqrstuvwxyz<br>abcdefghijklmnopqrstuvwxyz
abcdefghijklmnopqrstuvwxyz<br>abcdefghijklmnopqrstuvwxyz
abcdefghijklmnopqrstuvwxyz<br>abcdefghijklmnopqrstuvwxyz
abcdefghijklmnopqrstuvwxyz<br>abcdefghijklmnopqrstuvwxyz
abcdefghijklmnopqrstuvwxyz<br>abcdefghijklmnopqrstuvwxyz
abcdefghijklmnopqrstuvwxyz<br>abcdefghijklmnopqrstuvwxyz
abcdefghijklmnopqrstuvwxyz<br>abcdefghijklmnopqrstuvwxyz
abcdefghijklmnopqrstuvwxyz<br>abcdefghijklmnopqrstuvwxyz
abcdefghijklmnopqrstuvwxyz<br>abcdefghijklmnopqrstuvwxyz
abcdefghijklmnopqrstuvwxyz<br>abcdefghijklmnopqrstuvwxyz
abcdefghijklmnopqrstuvwxyz<br>abcdefghijklmnopqrstuvwxyz<TD>
```

continues

continued

```
<TD VALIGN=top WIDTH=50%>
<H1>HTML Style Sheets</H1>
<P CLASS=right>HTML style sheets are innovative primarily
in that they allow various different styles to be applied
to web pages by the author. Indeed, it could be said that
all web browsers already use a style to display text.
HTML style sheets are innovative primarily in that they
allow various different styles to be applied to web pages
by the author. Indeed, it could be said that all web
browsers already use a style to display text.
</P>
</TD>
</TABLE>
</BODY>
</HTML>
```

As you can see in the code, this HTML file is basically a table consisting of two cells, side by side, splitting the screen in the center. The left cell displays the white alphabet text on a black background. The right cell contains the actual paragraph text that uses a small 16-point margin-left value to keep the text away from the center dividing line. Notice that the margin value is based on the size of the right <TD> block that is the parent element of the <P> text.

The large headline is also part of the second, or right, table cell. The <H1> text is right justified, and the margin-left value of –75% allows it to cross the cell boundary and overlap the alphabet text. If the headline was part of the left cell, the text would be extended right off the screen.

You can elaborate further on this technique to create shadow-like effects for headline text. By replicating the <H1> element in the previous example twice and applying the .second and .third class identifiers, defined as follows, to the replicas, negative values for the margin-left and margin-top properties produce the results shown in Figure 11.4.

```
.second        {margin-left: -70%;
                margin-top: -25%;
                color: gray}

.third         {margin-left: -65%;
                margin-top: -25%;
                color: navy}
```

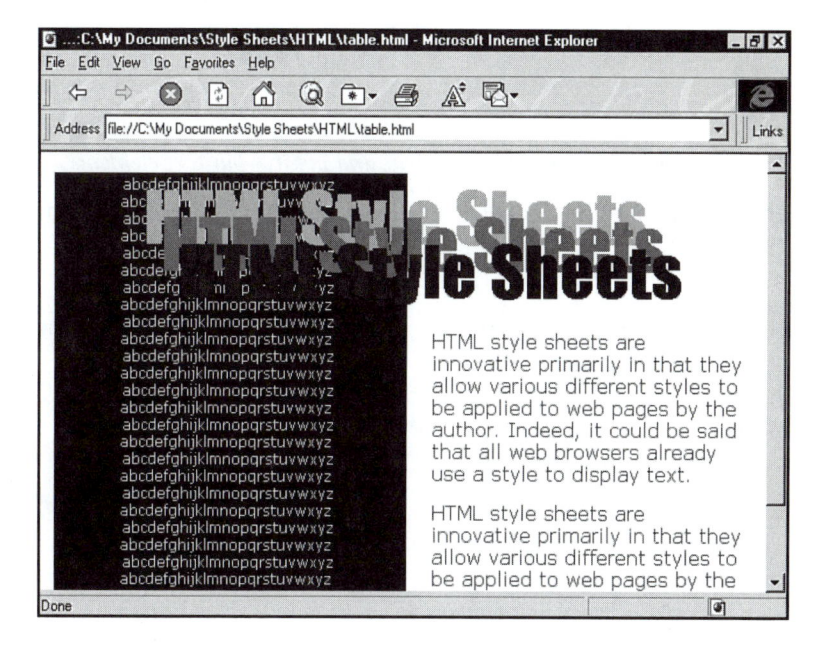

FIGURE 11.4 Applying negative values to the left and top margins produces a cascading shadow effect.

In this lesson, you learned how to apply margin properties to place HTML elements in specific locations on a web page. In the next lesson, you learn to modify your text layout with indents and justification.

12

SPECIFYING INDENTATION AND JUSTIFICATION VALUES

In this lesson, you learn how to indent and justify your text elements.

Indentation and justification are two more common desktop publishing functions that have thus far been difficult for web page authors. Styles now make them simple.

Indentation affects only the first line of a text block and moves its starting point inward a specified distance from the left margin. Justification is the selection of how text should be aligned, that is, how the words on a given line of text should be arranged in relation to the spaces between them.

The properties that control indentation and justification are text-indent and text-align, respectively. Both can be applied only to block elements and have no affect on inline tags such as <I> and <EM>. The value for the text-indent property is an absolute or relative measurement, while text-align takes keywords.

Both of these properties produce effects that are relatively subtle when compared to margin or font adjustments. However, they can lend an air of professionalism to a document and greatly increase its readability.

USING THE *TEXT-INDENT* PROPERTY

The text-indent property requires a value which indicates the distance that the first line of text is to be indented. The measurement can be in any of the scales that are typically supported by the CSS1 standard, such as:

- Points (pt)
- Inches (in)
- Centimeters (cm)
- Pixels (px)
- Ems (em)

A typical text-indent rule appears as follows:

```
P       {text-indent: .5in}
```

Relative values, in the form of percentages, can also be used with the text-indent property. The percentage is measured against the width of the parent element. If the parent has a substantially greater width than the child (due to the values of the child's margin properties, for example), you may have to apply a very small percentage to achieve the desired effect.

To demonstrate the effects of the text-indent property, create a file containing the following HTML code and name it **SAMPLE2.HTML**.

```
<HTML>
<HEAD>
<STYLE>
<!--
BODY        {font-size: 11pt;
            margin-left: 0in;
            background: white}

H2          {font-size: 24pt;
            font-family: Arial;
            margin-left: .5in;
            color: red}
```

```
P              {font-family: Verdana;
               margin-left: 1in;
               margin-right: 1in;
               color: darkblue}

.first         {text-indent: .5in}

.second        {text-indent: 36pt;
               margin-top: -.3in}

.third         {text-indent: 1.26cm;
               margin-top: -.3in}
-->
</STYLE>
</HEAD>
<BODY>
<H2>HTML Style Sheets</H2>

<P CLASS=first>HTML style sheets are innovative primarily
in that they allow various different styles to be applied
to web pages by the author. Indeed, it could be said that
all web browsers already use a style to display text.</P>

<P CLASS=second>A style is simply a collection of text
and layout attributes that can be selectively applied to
all or part of a document. The idea of grouping them
into a style allows the author to easily apply the same
collection of attributes to many different parts of a
document.</P>

<P CLASS=third>The HTML styles</SPAN> in Microsoft's
Internet Explorer 3.0 are based on a draft standard being
developed by the World Wide Web Consortium (W3C).</P>
</BODY>
<HTML>
```

You can see that the text-indent values for the three class selectors: .first, .second, and .third, all result in the same effect for the three paragraphs. Indents typically take small values, rarely more than an inch. Too great an indent is distracting and hampers readability. Indents are also inherited by the children of the elements to which they are applied.

Normally, the <P> tag forces a line break that clearly delineates paragraphs, but by applying negative margin-top values, you can create a continuous text block that uses indents to indicate the beginnings of the paragraphs, as shown in Figure 12.1.

TIP **Paragraph Breaks** Indents are only applied when paragraphs are broken by the application of separate <P> tags. A new paragraph that is the result of an inline break (such as when the <BR> tag is used) will not be indented by the text-align property.

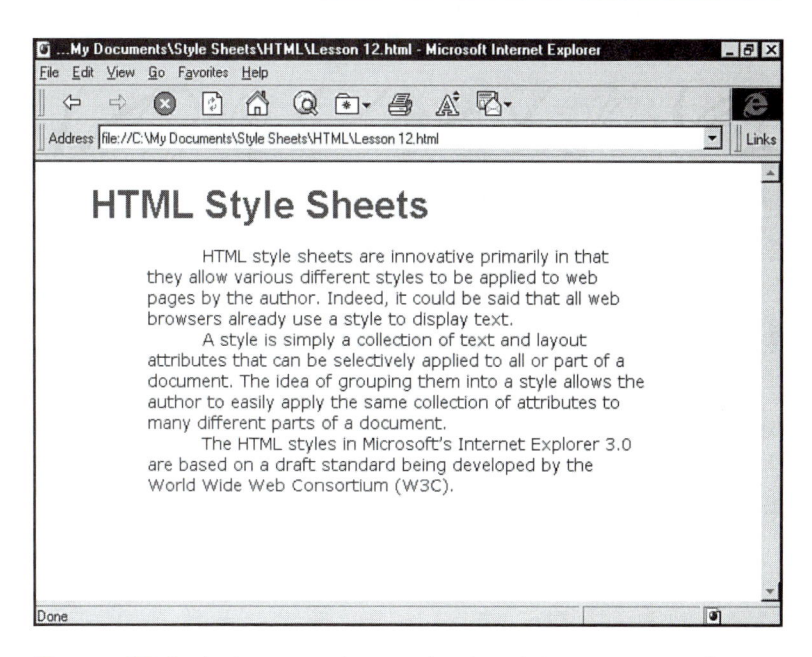

FIGURE 12.1 Indents can be used to break long streams of text into clearly visible paragraphs.

Indents can also have negative values, producing an *outdent* or a *hanging indent*. Adding a negative sign to the values of the three class selectors' text-indent properties produces the results shown in Figure 12.2.

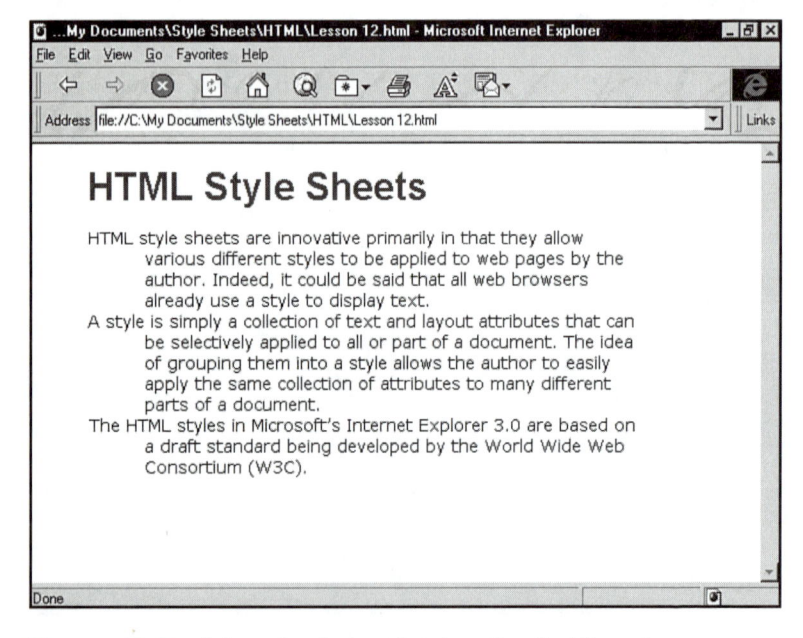

FIGURE 12.2   A hanging indent is when the first line of a paragraph extends to the left, beyond the margin.

USING THE *TEXT-ALIGN* PROPERTY

Use the text-align property to control the justification of a text block. Its value must be one of four keywords:

- left
- right
- center
- justify

 **Explorer Support** Internet Explorer 3.0 does not support the `justify` value for the `text-align` property.

When text is streamed between two margins, each line is filled until there is no room left to add another word. Because word lengths vary, there is usually a number of spaces left over between the last word and the margin.

Left justification places all of the leftover spaces at the right margin. Each line begins at the left margin and ends somewhere before the right margin. This is also known in the publishing trade as *ragged right*, due to the uneven edges at the right side of the page.

When those extra spaces are placed at the left margin, allowing the end of each line to touch the right margin, you have right justification. Center justification divides the extra spaces evenly at both ends of the line. Neither side meets the margin and the text is symmetrical through a center axis. Right and center justification should not be used for long text streams. The irregular left margin makes it difficult for the eye to find the beginning of each line.

Most printed books and periodicals use full justification, represented by the `justify` value. Fully justified text distributes the extra spaces as evenly as possible between the words on each line.

Full justification is not supported by Internet Explorer 3.0. Although this may seem like a serious shortcoming, you must realize that making fully justified text both attractive and readable is a difficult undertaking. Depending on the length of the lines and the lengths of the words, you can end up with a lot of empty space on each line, forcing you to leave large breaks between words.

This is why fully justified text is extremely reliant on good hyphenation. Hyphenating words allows more of the empty spaces on each line to be filled with parts of words. Desktop publishing programs usually have hyphenation dictionaries that are used to determine where hyphens can be correctly placed in particular words. Because web pages must adjust to fit a browser window and because there are no hyphenating tools for browsers, you are actually better off using left-justified text for long paragraphs.

For decorative use and for smaller blocks of text such as headlines, the use of right and center justification can be a powerful tool. By making a few modifications to the `margin` and `text-align` properties in the **SAMPLE2.HTML** file from Lesson 11 and removing the `text-indent` properties, the following <STYLE> block results, and you get a document that looks like Figure 12.3.

```
<STYLE>
<!--
BODY            {font-size: 11pt;
                background: white}

H2              {font-size: 24pt;
                font-family: Arial;
                text-align: center;
                color: red}

P               {font-family: Verdana;
                margin-left: .1in;
                margin-right: .1in;
                color: darkblue}

.first          {margin-right: 50%;
                text-align: right}

.second         {margin-top: -.3in;
                margin-left: 50%;
                text-align: left}

.third          {margin-top: -.3in;
                margin-left: 25%;
                margin-right: 25%;
                text-align: center}
-->
</STYLE>
```

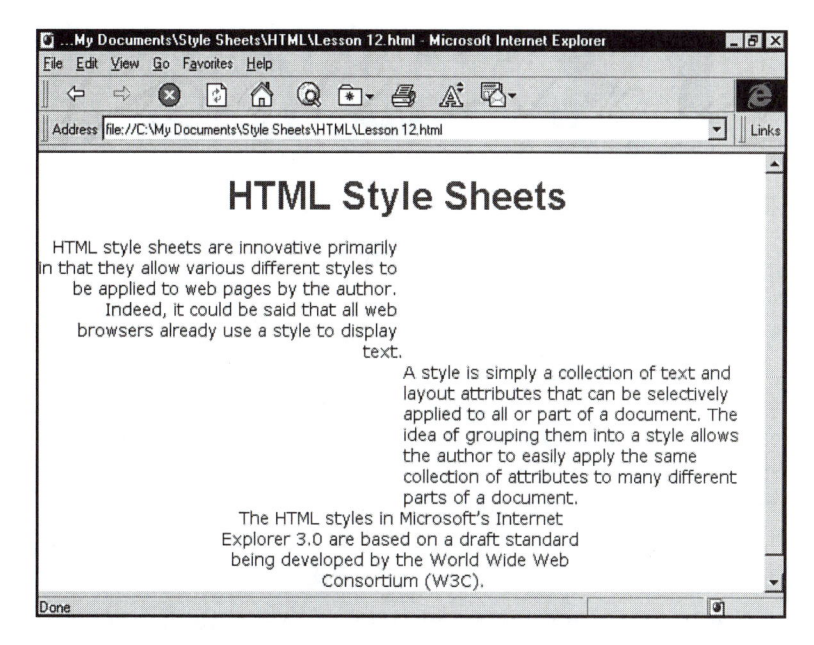

FIGURE 12.3 Varying text justification breaks up a page and can be used to create interesting layout effects.

In this lesson, you learned how to alter the appearance of text blocks using indents and justification. In the next lesson, you will learn to control the spaces between letters, words, and lines.

13

CONTROLLING WHITE SPACE

In this lesson, you learn how to modify the size of the spaces between letters, words, and lines of text.

Graphic designers and desktop publishers develop a keen eye for the details of how text is laid out on a page. Professional-quality page layout programs can often adjust page elements by increments as small as a thousandth of an inch. You can imagine the degree of frustration that results when these people are faced with the restraints imposed by HTML. HTML styles return some of these features to the hands of the web page author.

In past lessons, you learned how styles can return to the author control of functions that are normally set only in the browser software. In this lesson, you learn how to adjust settings that are unalterable by any other means, even at the browser level.

The amount of white space that is visible on a web page can be controlled with margin settings, as you have seen in Lesson 12. You can also use styles to control the white space within a block of text. The CSS1 standard includes properties that can modify the amount of space that is left between lines of text, between words, and between letters.

USING THE *LINE-HEIGHT* PROPERTY

In publishing circles, the space between lines of text is called *leading* (rhymes with bedding). The term originated during the days of manual typesetting when blanks made of lead were inserted between the lines of type to increase the space between them. Leading should not be confused with the line spacing feature of typewriters and word processors that allows you to double space your text (although it can be used for that purpose). Leading

usually refers to much finer adjustments, and the control provided by the line-height property permits you to specify leading
measurements in any of the scales supported by the CSS1 standard, including:

- Points (pt)

- Inches (in)

- Centimeters (cm)

- Pixels (px)

- Ems (em)

The line-height property would typically appear in a rule as
follows:

```
P       {line-height: 16pt}
```

You can only apply line-height to a block element (not to an
inline element). The measurement specified as the value for the
line-height property indicates the distance between the
baselines of a text block. The baseline is the invisible horizontal
rule on which a line of text rests (see Figure 13.1). A value of zero
causes all of the lines of text in the block to be placed on one rule,
stacked on top of one another. Therefore, the value of the line
height element should, at a minimum, be the same as the font-
size of the text, to avoid overlapping. Negative values are not
permitted.

The line-height value can also be expressed using relative measurements. A value of 100% causes a line-height equal to the
current font size. The CSS1 standard also defines the use of numerical values without any indication of the measurement scale
(such as a percent sign or a unit abbreviation). In this case, the
value represents a ratio to the current font size. A rule that appears as follows:

```
P       {line-height: 1.5}
```

would therefore result in a line-height of 1.5 times the current
font size. Line-height is an inherited property, but the relative
values behave in a slightly different manner. If you specify a

percentage as the value for the line-height property, the actual value of the current element is passed down to the child elements. This is typical inheritance behavior as defined by the CSS1 standard. If you specify a ratio as the value, however, it is the ratio that is passed down to the element's children, not the actual value.

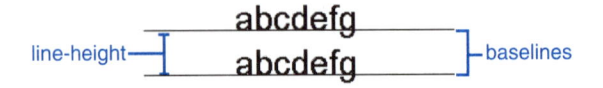

Figure 13.1   The line height of a block of text is the distance between baselines.

Explorer Support   Internet Explorer 3.0 does not support the use of ratio values in the line-height property as defined in the CSS1 standard. Numerical values without a unit of measurement are incorrectly interpreted as pixel values.

If you specify a line-height value of 150% on an element using a 12-point font, the children of that element inherit a line-height value of 18 points, whatever their font size. If you specify a value of 1.5, the line-height value of the child elements is 1.5 times their current font size.

To see the effect that leading can have on a text element, modify the <STYLE> block of the **SAMPLE2.HTML** file that you created in Lesson 12 by adding the line-height property to the declarations for the three class selectors called .first, .second, and .third, as shown:

```
<STYLE>
<!--
BODY          {font-size: 11pt;
        background: white}
```

```
H2              {font-size: 24pt;
                font-family: Arial;
                text-align: center;
                color: red}


P               {font-family: Verdana;
                margin-left: .1in;
                margin-right: .1in;
                color: darkblue}


.first            {margin-right: 50%;
                line-height: 24pt;
                text-align: right}


.second           {margin-left: 50%;
                line-height: 16pt;
                text-align: left}


.third            {margin-left: 25%;
                margin-right: 25%;
                line-height: 12pt;
                text-align: center}-->
</STYLE>
```

The result of the three different values is quite a different look for
each of the paragraphs (see Figure 13.2). Increasing the leading
causes a small block of text to attract more attention without an
increase in its size. You can also use leading to adjust the amount
of space occupied by a block of text, allowing you to even up
columns or create paragraphs that exactly correlate in size to a
graphic element.

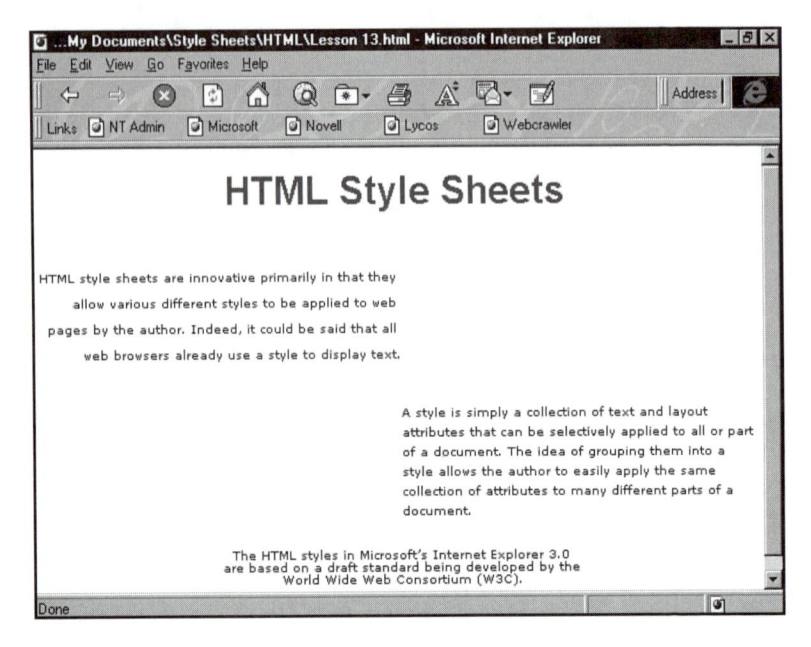

Figure 13.2 Minor changes in the `line-height` value can have a noticeable effect on the appearance of a text block.

Explorer Support You may notice that in Figure 13.2, the application of the `line-height` property has improperly caused the white space before and after each paragraph to be enlarged. Leading values should be applied only between two lines of text. This, plus the failure of the vertical margins to collapse properly (see Lesson 11), can cause excessively large inter-paragraph spaces. Until these issues are addressed, you can compensate for the problem by applying a smaller or negative value for the `margin-top` property.

Using the *word-spacing* Property

The publishing term that refers to the spacing between words and letters is *tracking*. Most desktop publishing software allows you to set a factor that adjusts the overall length of a line by spreading the letters slightly farther apart. The CSS1 standard, however, separates this function, and lets you adjust the spacing between words independently from the spacing between letters.

Just as the `line-height` property affects the distance between lines of text, the `word-spacing` property affects the distance between words. The `line-height` property can be applied to both block and inline text elements. A value can be specified by using any of the scales listed earlier in this lesson. The value corresponds to a distance that is added to the default space between each two words in the selected text. Percentage values are not permitted, but negative values are, to allow the reduction of space between words.

The typical values you would supply for the `word-spacing` property are very small. Too much space between words will make text more difficult to read. You can use larger values for display text, such as headlines, that can be made to match other architectural elements of your page in length without increasing the font size.

 **Explorer Support**   The `word-spacing` property is not supported by Internet Explorer 3.0.

USING THE *LETTER-SPACING* PROPERTY

You can adjust the distance between the letters within a word with the `letter-spacing` property. The concept should not be confused with *kerning*. Kerning is the adjustment of the space between individual pairs of letters to accommodate the design of a particular font. The `letter-spacing` property adjusts the spacing between all of the adjacent letters in a block of text by a specified amount, regardless of the font used or the letter pair. Theoretically, the `letter-spacing` property could be used to adjust kerning, but you would have to apply a style to each phonetic pair of letters in the document.

`letter-spacing` values are subject to the same restrictions as those for `word-spacing`. Any measurement scale can be used except percentages, and negative values are acceptable. Remember that the value you assign to the `letter-spacing` property is added to the default space between letters. If you are using a relatively large value for the `word-spacing` property, `letter-spacing` can also be applied to lessen what may be a jarring amount of space between words.

Explorer Support   The `letter-spacing` property is not supported by Internet Explorer 3.0.

The `letter-spacing` and `word-spacing` properties would typically appear in a rule as follows:

```
H1    {letter-spacing: 2pt;
      word-spacing: 4pt}
```

In this lesson, you learned how to adjust the spacing between lines, words, and letters. In the next lesson, you learn how to group style properties to save keystrokes and make your code easier to read and maintain.

GROUPING STYLE CODES

*In this lesson, you learn how to save time
and effort by combining the values and
selectors in your style rules.*

In the previous lessons, you learned to use over a dozen different
style properties to control the appearance of the text in your web
pages. You've also seen the `<STYLE>` blocks of your sample files
grow as you learned new properties and new techniques for applying them.

As you practice using style sheets to design web pages, you should
begin to consider the ways in which you can make your styles
more efficient. Writing HTML code in this way brings you a step
closer to actual programming. There are many ways to accomplish
the same end, but your goal is to find the most efficient one.

This lesson shows some coding shortcuts that can make the task
of defining your styles much easier. In fact, if you've gone
through all of the lessons up to this point, you may even be an-
noyed that they were not presented earlier. By concentrating first
on the individual properties, you had a chance to learn their full
capabilities and can now concentrate on their syntax.

GROUPING SELECTORS

Style rules are most efficient when they are fewer in number. One
way of minimizing your style code is to carefully organize your
selectors to avoid redundant properties. By grouping properties in
the combinations that are most often used, you can apply them
in more situations and leave other properties to be added by other
means.

For example, suppose you have a document that contains five
different sized headlines with various justifications. All of the
headlines require boldface Arial text, colored red. Rather than use

five separate rules which differ only in font size and justification, create a single rule containing the `font-weight`, `font-family`, and `color` properties and apply it to all five headline types. You can then apply the `font-size`, `justification`, and any other properties with a class selector, or some other technique.

If you find that you have to apply the same properties to several different selectors, you can specify the selectors in one rule, separating them with commas, as follows:

```
H1, H2, H3, H4, H5     {font-weight: bold;
    font-family: Ariel;
    color: red}
```

 **TIP** **Multiple Selectors**   When specifying multiple selectors in one rule, remember to separate them with commas or they will be interpreted as a contextual selector.

GROUPING *FONT* PROPERTIES

Another way to reduce code clutter is to group the values of related properties. You learned to use many different properties that affect fonts and their appearance. A rule that completely defines the look of a font may appear as follows:

```
P     {font-weight: bold;
    font-style: italic;
    font-size: 18pt;
    line-height: 22pt;
    font-family: "Times New Roman"}
```

In place of these five separate properties, the CSS1 standard defines a `font` property that is used to specify all of the values shown. The same five declarations, grouped together as the value of a single property, would appear as follows:

```
P     {font: bold italic 18pt/22pt "Times New Roman"}
```

The order of the values in a grouping of this type is critical. The font-weight and font-style values must precede the size measurements to prevent their keywords from being misinterpreted as part of a font-style name. Both of these properties are optional. The permitted keywords for the two are unique and allow the properties to be distinguished by their values alone.

The font-size and line-height values must appear in that order. If percentages are specified for these values, remember that the font-size value is relative to the size of the parent element, whereas the line-height value is relative to the font size of the current element.

Absolute measurements can use different scales. If only a single measurement value is specified, it is assumed to be a font size. A line-height value cannot be specified without an accompanying font size.

The font-family value must be enclosed in quotes if it contains one or more spaces, just as in the font-family property itself.

TIP — **Optional Values** The values for any properties omitted from a font declaration retain the values inherited by their parent element. They are not nullified or overridden by the inclusion of the font property.

Using the font property, you can consolidate the following rules from your **SAMPLE.HTML** file:

```
<STYLE>
<!--
H1          {font-family: Impact;
    font-size: 24pt;
    color: red;
    text-align: center}
```

```
H2.right              {font-family: Impact;
     font-size: 20pt;
     font-style: italic;
     color: blue;
     margin-left: 50%}

H2.center              {font-family: Impact;
     font-size: 20pt;
     font-style: italic;
     color: blue;
     margin-left: 25%;
     margin-right: 25%}

OL LI              {font-size: 110%;
     font-weight: bold}

OL OL LI              {font-size: 100%;
     font-weight: medium}

OL OL OL LI      {font-style: italic;
     font-size: 90%;
     font-weight: medium}
-->
</STYLE>
```

until they appear as follows:

```
<STYLE>
<!--
H1              {font: 24pt Impact;
     color: red;
     text-align: center}

H2.right              {font: italic 20pt Impact;
     color: blue;
     margin-left: 50%}
```

```
H2.center          {font: italic 20pt Im-
pact;
     color: blue;
     margin-left: 25%;
     margin-right: 25%}


OL LI              {font: bold 110%}


OL OL LI              {font: medium 100%}


OL OL OL LI        {font: medium italic 90%}
-->
</STYLE>
```

GROUPING *MARGIN* PROPERTIES

The properties used to specify the margin sizes for the four sides of a text block can also be grouped into a single declaration. The `margin` property takes up to four values, representing the `margin-top`, `margin-bottom`, `margin-left`, and `margin-right` properties respectively, as shown:

```
P      {margin: 1in 1in .5in .5in}
```

If you specify only one measurement for the value, the measurement is used for all four margins. If two or three measurements are specified, the missing values are taken from their opposite sides. This rule:

```
P      {margin: 1in .5in}
```

is equivalent to the first example above. The 1-inch value is applied to the top and bottom, and .5 inches to the left and right sides. A declaration with three measurements, such as:

```
P      {margin: 1in .5in 1in}
```

would again produce the same results. The first measurement would set the top margin; the second, the right; the third, the bottom; and the value for the left margin would be taken from the right.

Explorer Support   Since Internet Explorer 3.0 does not support the `margin-bottom` property, a `margin` property with three measurements would represent the `top`, `left`, and `right` margin values, respectively.

In this lesson, you learned how to reduce code clutter by grouping `font` and `margin` values into single properties. In the next lesson, you learn how to specify colors for the text and backgrounds of your pages.

Specifying Text and Background Values

In this lesson, you learn how to add visual appeal to your web pages by applying colors to the text and backgrounds of your HTML elements.

The creative use of color is one area of web page design that has surpassed the print publishing medium. Four-color printing processes are so much more expensive than simple monochrome techniques that color printed pages are usually reserved only for situations that demand them. When you are serving documents over the World Wide Web, however, a colored pixel costs no more than a black one, so authors are free to create color effects that would normally not be attempted in printed media.

Of course, there is a distinct backlash to this newly found freedom. Just as digital font technology tends to entice over-zealous designers to use too many different fonts on a single page (producing the *ransom note effect*), the sudden availability of color may lead some web designers to excess.

Style sheets might even be guilty of fueling this phenomenon because they provide new capabilities. It has always been possible to globally assign colors to a page's text and background, but with styles, you can now apply a color to the text or background of any HTML element.

One of the first practical uses is to create separate sections within a document that are distinguishable by their background color. Many of the style sheet samples, already available on the web, use a table to create an enclosure within the <BODY> of a document that contains the page's entire contents. By making the table somewhat smaller than the canvas and using contrasting colors for the <BODY> background and the table cells, the document can easily take on the appearance of a page, as shown in Figure 15.1.

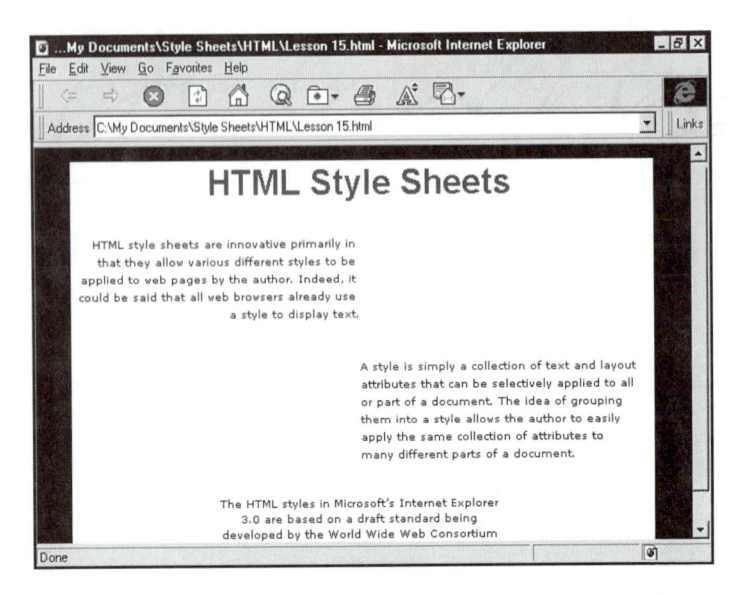

Figure 15.1 Styles permit backgrounds of different HTML elements to be assigned different colors.

This technique is used to create other designs as well. After creating table cells with different background colors, you can use colored headline and paragraph text elements with negative margin values to make them span the cells.

Individual text selections consisting of either block or inline elements can also be assigned different colors. You can contrast your headlines from your body text, or use color as an alternative to bold or italics to emphasize inline text selections.

Using the *color* Property

It has long been possible to assign a color value to a web page's text by using the TEXT= attribute in the <BODY> tag. This attribute causes all of the text on the page to be the same color. An exception is for link text that you learn about in Lesson 17, "Using Pseudo-Elements and Pseudo-Classes." Recent additions to the HTML language now permit you to set the color of any selected text with the <FONT> tag.

There is nothing about style sheets that stops you from using these features. You can replace the TEXT= attribute and your inline <FONT> tags with a style that uses the color property to assign a color value to text. You can apply the same property to any other element in a web page to permit variation of text colors.

The color property is notated like any other CSS1 property. It takes a value that represents the desired color, by using one of the following notations:

- A keyword representing one of the 16 basic Windows colors

- An RGB value in hexadecimal format

- An RGB value in decimal format

A rule containing the color property will appear like one of the following (all of which specify the same shade of blue):

```
H1      {color: blue}
H1      {color: #00F}
H1      {color: #0000FF}
H1      {color: rgb(0,0,255)}
H1      {color: rgb(0%, 0%, 100%)}
```

The color property is inherited. Unstyled text displays using the default browser color (which is black), or a color specified using the <BODY> or <FONT> tag.

SPECIFYING KEYWORD VALUES

The simplest way to specify a color value is to name the color desired but this also provides the most limited range of colors. The keywords that are permitted represent the basic 16-color VGA palette of the Windows operating systems. They are as follows:

black	navy	maroon	blue
aqua	purple	gray	green
fuchsia	lime	olive	red
silver	teal	yellow	white

SPECIFYING RGB VALUES

The other, far more flexible method for defining colors is to specify the individual RGB (red, green, and blue) values that can be combined to form the final color. The number of colors that can be created by adjusting the proportions of red, green, and blue is virtually infinite. The limiting factors are the method by which you notate the proportions and the capability of the medium on which they are displayed. You can freely mix RGB and keyword color values in a document, as needed. However, if your readers are viewing your pages using the standard 16-color VGA Windows video driver, you should stick to colors named by keywords.

You can specify RGB values for the color property as hexadecimal or standard decimal numbers. Hexadecimal is the standard form that you may have used when specifying color values in traditional HTML codes.

A hexadecimal color specification consists of three or six digits with 16 possible values from 0 (zero) to F. The digits are divided equally into red, green, and blue (in that order), with F being the highest proportion of that color. In the sample color rules shown earlier, the second and third examples both indicate the same blue color.

`#00F` indicates a full measure of blue, with no green or red. With a single digit, there are sixteen possible gradations for each color element, or 4096 possible color combinations.

`#0000FF` indicates the same blue, but uses two digits for each color, permitting 256 possible gradations for each. This increases the number of possible colors using this system to 16,777,216. You can either use the single- or double-digit notation for any color property, although double-digit is more common.

For example, the double-digit hexadecimal values for the 16 VGA colors are shown in the following table:

Color	Hexidecimal Value	Color	Hexidecimal Value
black	000000	navy	000080
maroon	800000	blue	0000FF
aqua	00FFFF	purple	800080

Color	Hexidecimal Value	Color	Hexidecimal Value
gray	808080	green	008000
fuchsia	FF00FF	lime	00FF00
olive	808000	red	FF0000
silver	C0C0C0	teal	008080
yellow	FFFF00	white	FFFFFF

The problem with this notation system is that most people are not accustomed to working with hexadecimal numbers and they are not familiar with the RGB color scale. One way around this problem is to find a tool that allows you to mix colors while providing the hexadecimal RGB values for the result, such as the example shown in Figure 15.2.

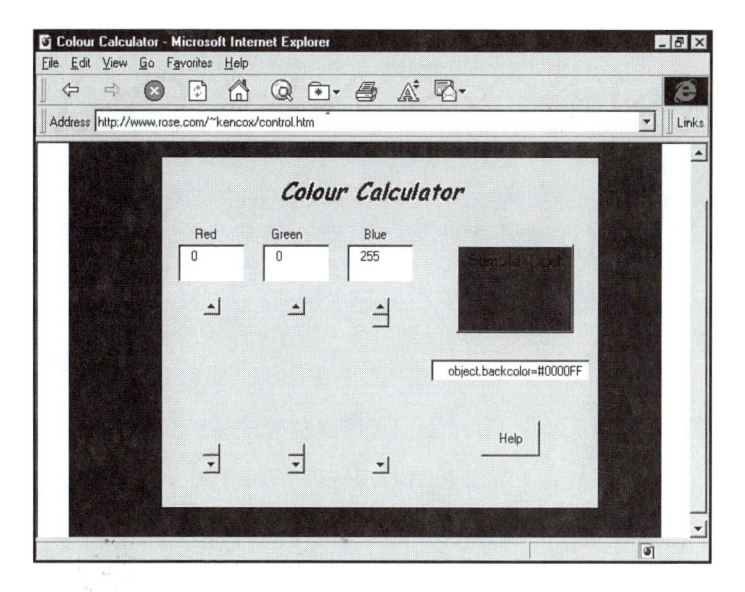

Figure 15.2   You can find this simple, but serviceable, ActiveX tool for mixing RGB colors live on the web at **www.rose.com/~kencox/control.htm**.

The same color precision is provided by the decimal notation method because 256 is the decimal equivalent of the hexadecimal

FF. You can also use percentages that provide a lesser degree of control but are more than adequate.

There are many more applications that display RGB color values as decimals or percentages than there are hexadecimal ones. Even the Paint program included with Windows 95 and Windows NT 4.0 can display them. To do this, select Edit Colors from the Options menu and then click the Define Custom Colors button.

Explorer Support Internet Explorer 3.0 does not support the notation of color values in the RGB() decimal or percentage formats.

Unfortunately, the enormous number of colors that you can specify in your styles doesn't mean that the browser can display them all properly. When you want to be certain that your readers are seeing exactly the same colors that you have selected, you are limited by the Internet Explorer to a palette of 216 colors. Color values not on the Explorer palette display using the nearest available palette color.

Color Palette A web page displaying all of the colors in the Internet Explorer Color Palette, along with their RGB values, can be found at **www.microsoft.com/workshop/ author/roberth/set1/iecolors.htm**.

SPECIFYING A BACKGROUND COLOR

The same color notation techniques used on text are also used to apply color to the background on which the text is placed. You can apply the background property to any HTML element, block, or inline, as follows:

```
P       {background: red}
P       {background: #FF0000}
```

The background property is not inherited by child objects. However, a child object has a default background value of transparent, which allows the parent's background to show through.

When a background color is applied to a block element, the CSS1 standard specifies that the color should extend through the padding of the block, and up to the rectangular border (the color of which is set with the `border` property).

Internet Explorer 3.0 does not support the `padding` property defined by the CSS1 standard so background colors assigned to certain block elements (such as <P> elements) cover only the immediate area on which there is actual text. This leaves irregularly shaped blocks instead of rectangular ones (see Figure 15.3).

Additional leading added by the `line-height` property also can cause breaks in the background color between lines, as shown in Figure 15.3's second paragraph. Elements that have established boundaries, such as table cells, display backgrounds properly.

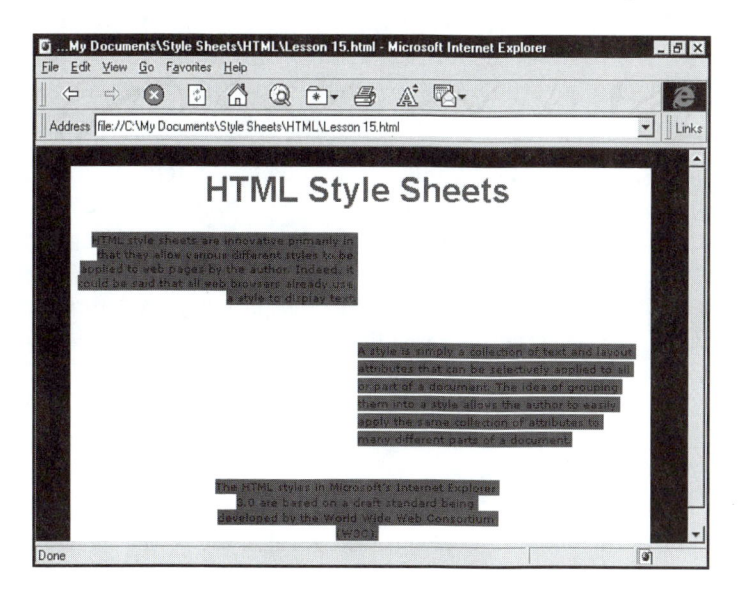

Figure 15.3   Current support of the CSS1 standard by the Internet Explorer causes the background property to be applied improperly.

In this lesson, you learned how to assign color values to the text and background of your documents. In the next lesson, you learn how to create more elaborate background effects.

Lesson 16
USING BACKGROUND GRAPHICS

In this lesson, you learn how to create backgrounds for your web pages using graphic files in new and exciting ways.

In the last lesson, you saw how the traditional HTML technique of assigning a background color to your web pages has been enhanced by the use of styles to assign backgrounds to individual elements. This lesson demonstrates how the other standard background technique, the use of external graphic files, has also been enhanced.

Typically, a graphic background is applied by referencing the URL of a small GIF or JPG file in the <BODY> tag, using the BACKGROUND= attribute. You can continue to use the standard method of assigning the background a color with a <BODY> attribute and also apply styles to other elements. The background property, as defined in the CSS1 standard, permits you to reference graphic files in the same way and to exercise far more control over them than you can with traditional HTML.

SPECIFYING BACKGROUND URLs

To specify the URL for a background graphic file, add a value to the background property that consists of the URL plus the file's location, in parentheses, as follows:

```
BODY        {background: URL(pattern.gif}
BODY        {background: URL(/graphics/pattern.gif)}
BODY        {background: URL(http://www.mycorp.com/graphics/
            pattern.gif)}
```

Use the standard Internet http notation for the URL within the parentheses to provide either a complete or relative path to the desired file.

As with values specifying colors, a background graphic can be applied to any HTML element and is subject to the same behavior described in Lesson 15. By default, a graphic supplied for a background is tiled to fill the entire space occupied by the background, repeating a small graphic like that shown in Figure 16.1 to create a background pattern for a whole page.

FIGURE 16.1   By tiling the image, a tiny graphic file fills the entire browser screen very quickly.

The same technique used in Lesson 15 to create the look of a page on the browser screen can be used with a background graphic to create quite a different effect. To do this, modify your **SAMEPL2.HTML** file from Lesson 13 to appear as follows:

```
<HTML>
<HEAD>
<STYLE>
<!--
BODY     {font-size: 11pt;
             margin-left: 0in;
             background: black}

TD       {background: URL(\windows\Black Thatch.bmp)}

H2       {font-size: 24pt;
             font-family: Arial;
             text-align: center;
             color: red}

P        {font-family: Verdana;
             font-size: 14pt
             margin-left: .1in;
             margin-right: .1in;
             color: white}
```

```
.first    {margin-right: 50%;
           line-height: 16pt;
           text-align: right}

.second   {margin-left: 50%;
           line-height: 16pt;
           text-align: left}

.third    {margin-left: 25%;
           margin-right: 25%;
           line-height: 16pt;
           text-align: center}
-->
</STYLE>
</HEAD>
<BODY>
<CENTER>
<TABLE WIDTH=90% BORDER=none>
<TD>
<H2>HTML Style Sheets</H2>
<P CLASS=first>HTML style sheets are innovative primarily in
that they allow various different styles to be applied to web
pages by the author. Indeed, it could be said that all web
browsers already use a style to display text.</P>
<P CLASS=second>A style is simply a collection of text and
layout attributes that can be selectively applied to all or
part of a document. The idea of grouping them into a style
allows the author to easily apply the same collection of
attributes to many different parts of a document.</P>
<P CLASS=third>The HTML styles</SPAN> in Microsoft's Internet
Explorer 3.0 are based on a draft standard being developed by
the World Wide Web Consortium (W3C).</p>
</TD>
</TABLE>
</CENTER>
</BODY>
</HTML>
```

TIP

Background Image Files   The **Black Thatch.bmp** file used in the **SAMPLE2.HTML** code is one of the wallpaper bitmaps that ships with the Windows 95 and Windows NT 4.0 operating systems. It can be found in the Windows home directory if you selected the Desktop Wallpaper item in the Accessories group during the operating system installation.

Notice that the three paragraphs in the `<BODY>` section have been enclosed within a single-celled table that occupies 90% of the browser's width. This creates a rectangle within the rectangle of the canvas, and by applying the `background` property to the `<TD>` element, the tiny graphic shown in Figure 16.1 is repeated to fill the page, as shown in Figure 16.2.

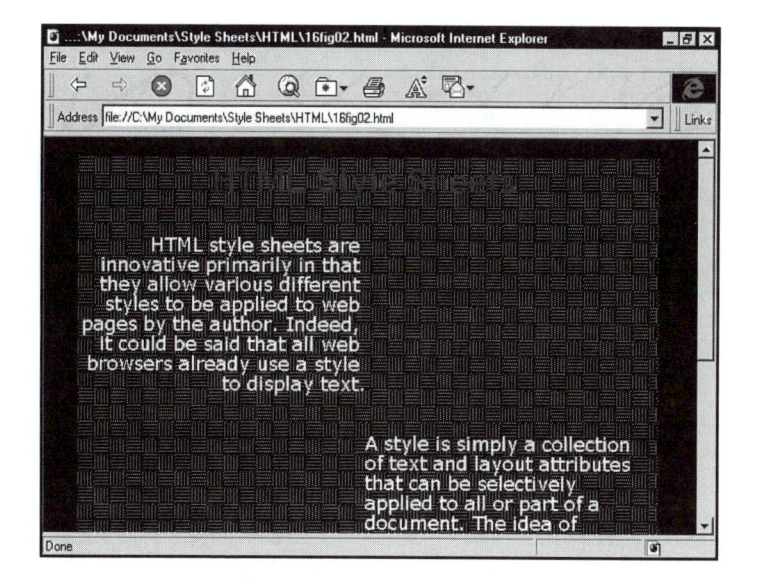

Figure 16.2   A background graphic applied to a table can create a background pattern without filling the entire screen.

CONTROLLING REPETITION

Although a background graphic is tiled by default, the `background` property permits you to control the way the image is repeated or can prevent any repetition at all. The tiling pattern of a standard background stretches along two axes, the x-axis that runs horizontally across the screen, and the y-axis that runs vertically. The repetitive behavior of a URL specified as a background is controlled by adding one of the following additional values to the background property:

- `repeat` (default)   Causes the graphic image to be repeated along both axes

- `no-repeat`   Prevents any repetition of the graphic image

- `repeat-x`   Causes the graphic image to be repeated along the x-axis only (horizontally)

- `repeat-y`   Causes the graphic image to be repeated along the y-axis only (vertically)

The ability to control the repetition of the image allows web pages to be designed with effects that are more easily scaleable to browsers running at different resolutions.

One fairly common effect is to use a background to simulate the look of an open notebook page on the desktop. By tiling an image, the spiral binding of the notebook is made to extend down the left side of the page. When done in the traditional way, the graphic file must extend over the entire width of the screen, even though the actual image is only on the far left side, in order to prevent it from repeating horizontally. Because readers run their browsers at different screen resolutions and different window sizes, it is difficult to accommodate them all with one graphic file.

With styles, you can use a graphic file containing only the image, such as that shown in Figure 16.3 and force it to repeat down the vertical axis on the left side of the page only. This way, the right side of the page can expand to any size and support both high and low resolution displays.

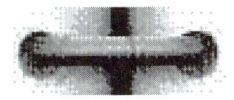

FIGURE 16.3   Simple images like this one repeat with greater control using styles.

To do this, you would change the rule for the <TD> tag in your **SAMPLE2.HTML** file to appear as follows:

```
TD              {background: URL(notebook.jpg) repeat-y white}
```

The result is the page shown in Figure 16.4. Notice how the tiled background is restricted to the confines of the table and how a color value (white, in this case) can be supplied along with the URL. You can also use any of the RGB formats discussed in Lesson 15 to specify the color that appears in the areas of the background that are not covered by the graphic image.

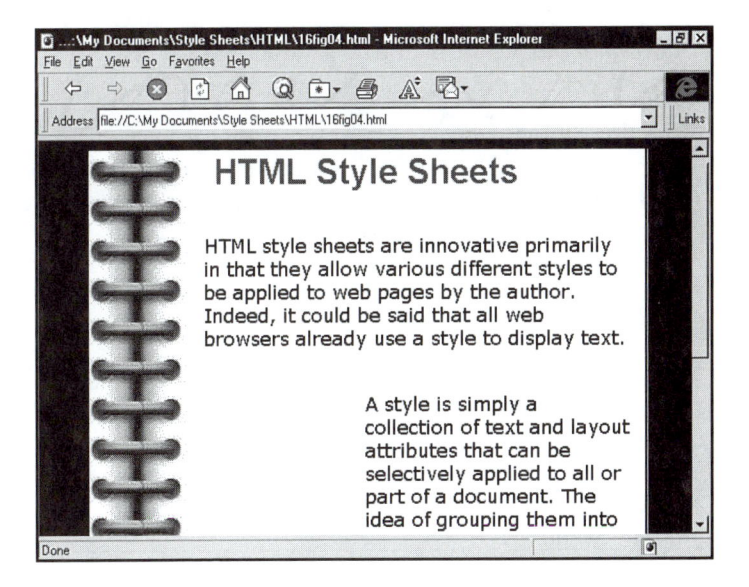

FIGURE 16.4   Repetition of a background image can be restricted to the horizontal or vertical axis.

POSITIONING GRAPHICS

When you change the `background` property's repetition behavior, as in the last example, you often create a situation in which the image does not occupy the entire space devoted to the background. When you use a single instance of an image on the page, or repeat it along one axis, you can add additional values to the background property that permit you to place the image in any location that you wish. Without additional values, the image is placed in the upper left corner of the background.

Image placement is controlled by two values representing the distance from the upper left corner along the x-axis (horizontal) and the y-axis (vertical). The distance can be expressed using percentages, keywords, or length measurements. Relative measurements are computed against the size of the background containing the image(s).

Location values should appear at the end of the background property declaration. A single value assigns the same distance to both axes. Two values express the horizontal and vertical distances, respectively.

For example, the following rule places a single instance of the graphic image 25% of the way in from the left margin and 50% of the way down the page from the top margin, as shown in Figure 16.5.

```
TD          {background: URL(notebook.jpg) no-repeat white
             25% 50%}
```

You can also use keywords to specify the distances—the values are shown in the following table:

HORIZONTAL (X-AXIS)

Keyword	Distance
left	0%
center	50%
right	100%

Vertical (Y-axis)

Keyword	Distance
top	0%
middle	50%
bottom	100%

You can also specify absolute distances using any of the standard measurement scales accepted by the CSS1 standard (inches, centimeters, points, ems, and pixels).

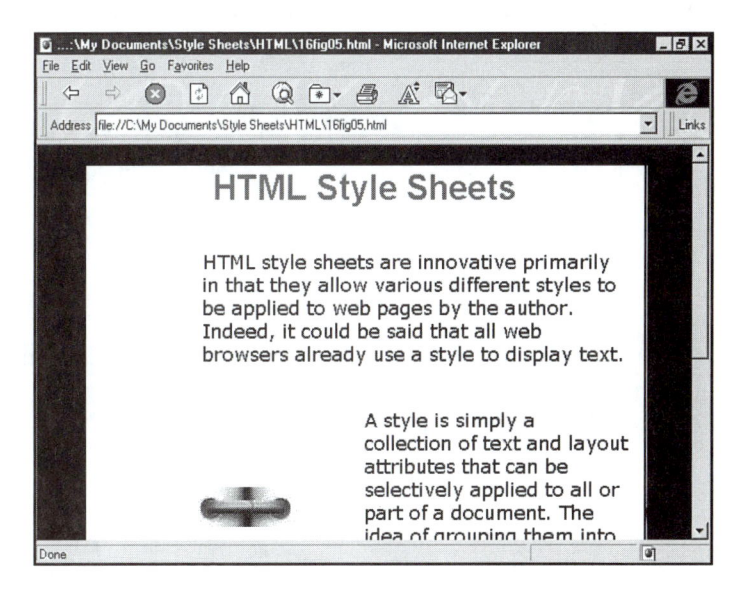

Figure 16.5   For the first time, style sheets enable you to locate a background graphic on a page with absolute precision.

 **Explorer Support**   Internet Explorer 3.0 does not support the use of absolute measurements in the placement of background graphics. Percentages and keywords, however, are supported.

Scrolling Graphics

Another feature of the `background` property is the ability to control whether an image scrolls with the text in the foreground (which is the default), or remains fixed on the screen while the text scrolls over it. With this feature, you can place a single logo or other image in the center of a web page and have it remain stationary as readers scroll through the contents of the documents.

To stop a background from scrolling, add the fixed keyword to the background declaration anywhere after the URL specification. The scroll keyword triggers the opposite behavior.

 **TIP** **Image Scrolling** The ability to fix an image to a specific spot is only available in relation to the overall canvas (that is, the entire area of the browser occupied by the document). The fixed keyword, therefore, is only effective when used in a background declaration applied to the <BODY> tag.

This watermark technique is a subtle but effective way of keeping the reader's attention on a company name or trademark, without the need for the endless repetition of tiling.

USING PSEUDO-ELEMENTS AND PSEUDO-CLASSES

Certain elements of an HTML document can be assigned a unique appearance based on their function, not on their location within the document, or on other factors defined by the browser. These are known as *pseudo-classes* and *pseudo-elements* and do not appear as part of the HTML code. The browser, however, still recognizes them by other means and treats them like actual classes and elements.

The most common example of the pseudo-class is evident in the way that browsers display link text. All web users are familiar with the blue, underlined text that identifies a hyperlink in most standard browser configurations. The link text itself is identified in the HTML document by the use of the <A> tag with the HREF= attribute. However, you have probably also noticed that the color of the link text changes after you visit the link's URL.

Typically, the text changes from a bright blue color to a duller aqua, although the colors and text decorations that are used are configurable in most browsers. This color reverts back to its original appearance after a length of time that the browser specifies.

This change in state is not apparent in the HTML code, but the CSS1 standard permits you to specify pseudo-classes in your selectors for the <A> tag that respond to the various link states that the browser defines.

Pseudo-Class A pseudo-class is a means of selecting certain text in an HTML document and is based on other external conditions applied by the web browser, not on the HTML code of the document itself.

Modifying the Appearance of Links

The CSS1 standard defines three pseudo-classes that relate to the state of links in a web browser. These differ from actual classes (like those discussed in Lesson 4) because there is no indication of them in the body of HTML documents themselves. They can, however, be addressed by styles in nearly the same way as normal classes.

The pseudo-classes for the <A> tag are applicable only when the HREF= attribute is included in the tag. This is only when <A> is used to actually indicate a link. The <A> tags with the NAME= attribute, which are used to create targets for internal document links, are not affected by pseudo-classes.

The three pseudo-classes recognized by the CSS1 standard are as follows:

- A:link   Used to address anchor links that have not been visited by the web browser in a specified length of time.

- A:visited   Used to address anchor links that have been visited by the web browser within a specified length of time.

- A:active   Used to address the anchor link that is currently being activated by the client operating the web browser (Netscape only).

Active Links   The A:active pseudo-class applies only to the link on which the user is currently clicking the mouse. It is therefore applicable only during the brief transitory period while the link is being selected. Only the Netscape browser defines a separate color for this state. The A:active pseudo-class will, therefore, have no effect in the Internet Explorer.

These pseudo-classes are specified as selectors in style rules (just as any other class selector would be) except that a colon is used between the selector and the class instead of a period. Typical rules that alter the appearance of anchor links appear as follows:

```
A:link      {font-size: 130%;
            color: white;
            background: black;
            text-decoration: none}

A:visited {font-weight: bold;
            text-decoration: none;
            font-style: italic;
            color: red;
            background: white}
```

Notice that the `text-decoration` property is applied with a `none` value. This overrides the underlining that is part of the browser default style for anchor links.

To see the effect of these styles, add the rules shown above to the <STYLE> block of your **SAMPLE2.HTML** file and add some anchor links to Internet sites to the paragraph text of the document. When you load the document in your browser, the links should appear like the words **HTML style sheets** in Figure 17.1 with white text on a black background. If you follow one of the links to its target, and hit the back button to return to your page, you should see that the link has changed to red, bold italic text on a white background, like the words **Internet Explorer 3.0** in the Figure.

 **TIP**   **Displaying Properties**   In order for your links to display the properties assigned to the `A:visited` selector, they must point to files on another machine. Links to pages on a local drive will never be shown as "visited."

You can also combine pseudo-classes with other style techniques to isolate link text in certain areas of a document. Define contextual selectors with the `A:link` or `A:visited` as one of the elements, in the usual manner. A pseudo-class selector can also be used along with a real class selector, as long as the real class selector is specified in the rule before the pseudo-class. This would appear as follows:

```
A.external:link          {font-size: 130%;
    color: white;
    background: black;
    text-decoration: none}
```

The style rule shown would be applied only to text that was contained within anchor tags that included both an HREF= attribute and a CLASS=external attribute, as follows:

```
<A HREF="http://www.microsoft.com" CLASS=external>Internet
Explorer 3.0</A>
```

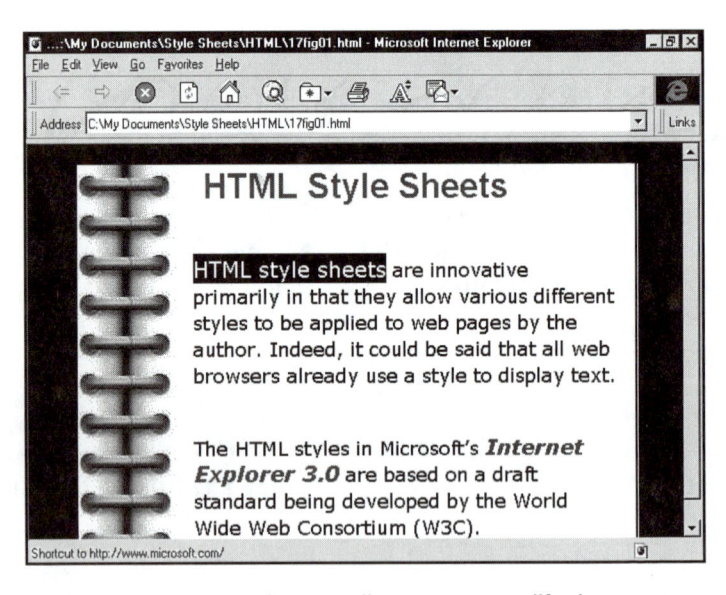

Figure 17.1   Pseudo-classes allow you to modify the appearance of hyperlinks in your documents.

Modifying the Appearance of Pseudo-Elements

In addition to pseudo-classes, you can also apply styles to pseudo-elements. A pseudo-element identifies a portion of another element according to the way the browser presents it. As with pseudo-classes, there is nothing in a document's HTML code to indicate the existence of these structures.

The CSS1 standard recognizes two pseudo-elements to which styles can be applied: `first-line` and `first-letter`. The `first-line` pseudo-element refers to the first line of text in any element as the browser displays it. Because its value can be changed simply by resizing the browser window, this structure cannot be coded in HTML.

 **Explorer Support**   Internet Explorer 3.0 does not support the use of pseudo-elements as selectors but does support pseudo-classes.

Style properties that are defined for the `first-line` pseudo-element only apply to the first line of any text element. If you adjust the margins or the font size or make any other changes that affect the length of the line, the selected text also changes.

You can create interesting effects by applying a style that emphasizes the first line of a paragraph using a different color, a larger font size, or bold or italic text, as shown in Figure 17.2.

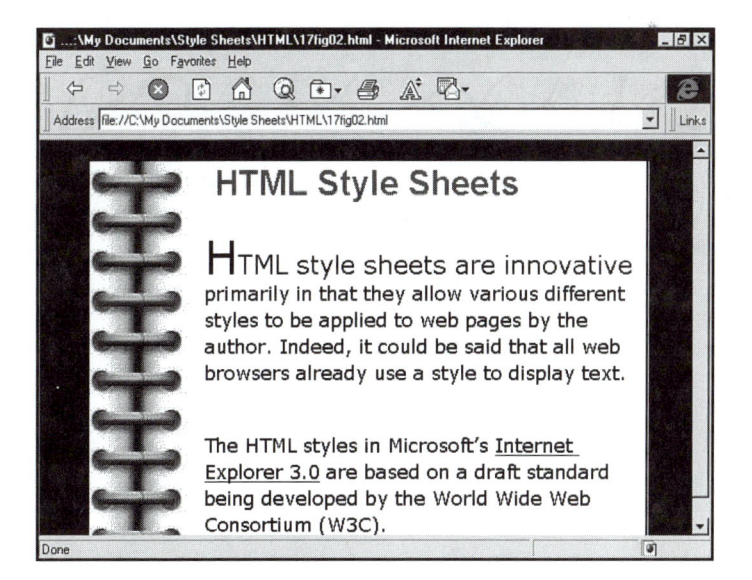

Figure 17.2   Pseudo-elements allow you to apply styles to specific parts of other elements.

The first-letter pseudo-element performs the same function for the first letter of any element. This can be used to emulate the technique of using a large and elaborate capital letter to begin a paragraph or page.

Pseudo-element selectors are notated in style definitions much like pseudo-classes, as shown:

```
P:first-line      {font-size: 150%}

P:first-letter     {font-size: 400%;
     font-family:  Zapf Chancery ,  Times New
Roman , cursive}
```

Pseudo-classes and pseudo-elements are subject to the same rules of inheritance as other elements. If desired, both of these rules can be applied to the same text element. The P:first-letter element would behave like the child of the P:first-line element.

Pseudo-elements can be used in contextual and class selectors, just like pseudo-classes, except that the pseudo-element must be the last of the multiple selectors specified in a contextual selector, as shown:

```
P.heading:first-letter     {font-style: bold}
DIV P:first-line           {font-size: 150%}
```

In this lesson, you learned how to apply styles to special selectors that are not revealed by a document's HTML code. In the next lesson, you learn how to use style definitions that are stored in a separate file.

Using Style Sheet Files

LESSON 18

In this lesson, you learn how to apply styles to HTML documents that are stored in an external file.

In Lesson 1 you learned there are three ways of applying styles to HTML documents: linking, embedding, and inserting them inline. Up until this point, you have dealt only with embedded styles. In this lesson and the next, you learn to use the other methods.

The technique of embedding styles implies a web authoring paradigm that centers around the individual document. You have learned ways to reduce the amount of coding needed to produce an HTML file by applying styles efficiently. The creation of less specific style rules that can be applied in more places leads to documents that are smaller in size and easier to maintain.

This philosophy extends beyond the single document. Style rules that apply to several different text selections on one web page can probably be used in other documents as well. Linking styles take the same style definitions that embed in a single document and store them in a separate file. The file can then be accessed by many different HTML documents.

This capability can move the primary emphasis of your web authoring effort from the document to the web site itself. If you create your styles with the overall appearance of your entire site in mind, you can dramatically reduce the repetitive coding chores, as well as create a consistent and unified look for your site.

You can also consider the advantages of external style sheets by reversing the equation. Instead of servicing many documents with one style sheet, it is possible to associate a single document with several different style sheets. This provides the reader with a choice of styles to suit the limitations of their medium or their particular preference.

You could create style sheets that support different designs for the same documents, full-color versus monochrome displays, high- versus low bandwidth connections, and even new technologies currently under development, such as speech synthesis equipment for nonvisual web access.

The possibilities are endless, but style sheets are still an emerging technology and development is ongoing. Internet Explorer 3.0 provides basic support for linked style sheets, but does not include the mechanisms for allowing the reader to select a style or combine styles from multiple sheets.

CREATING STYLE SHEETS

A style sheet is nothing more than an ASCII file that contains style rules just like those you embed in HTML documents. You can take either of the sample files that you created while working on the other lessons in this book, copy all of the code between the <STYLE> tags to a new file, and make an effective style sheet.

 **Explorer Support**   When you are creating a style sheet from a document with embedded styles, the <STYLE> tags themselves and any other extraneous HTML codes should be omitted—they can cause the Internet Explorer to process the style rules incorrectly.

Once you have created a style sheet, save it to a file with a CSS extension. It can then be placed on your web site at any location that is accessible to your readers. You will be linking your HTML documents to the style sheets using standard URLs, so you can either dedicate a directory to your style sheets or store them with the HTML documents themselves.

APPLYING STYLE SHEET FILES

The CSS1 standard defines two methods of linking style sheets to HTML documents—using the <LINK> tag and by the @import function. The intention is to provide two ways of specifying multiple style sheet files for two different purposes.

- <LINK>   Provides the means for the author to specify multiple files that the browser uses to assemble a menu of alternate style sheets for the reader.

- @import   Provides the means for one or more style sheet files to be specified by the author, their contents are combined for application to the HTML document.

 **Explorer Support**   Internet Explorer 3.0 does not support the use of the @import function or the use of multiple <LINK> tags pointing to style sheet files at this time.

Using the <*LINK*> Tag

The <LINK> tag is an HTML 3 convention that creates a hyperlink from an HTML document to another file type. The use of <LINK> to import style definitions from separate style sheet files is mentioned in the CSS1 standard and defined more fully in a document called **HTML3 and Style Sheets**. This document was developed by the World Wide Web Consortium.

<LINK> requires several attributes when applying style sheets. Its syntax appears as follows:

```
<LINK TITLE="color"  REL=stylesheet
HREF="http://www.mycorp.com/styles/sheet1.css"
TYPE="text/css">
```

The REL= attribute informs the browser that the linked file is a style sheet, HREF= specifies the URL of the style sheet file itself, and the TYPE= attribute supplies the Internet Media (MIME) type of the file. The TITLE= attribute supplies the name for the linked stylesheet that will be used when the browser constructs a style sheet selection menu.

TIP

MIME Types The inclusion of the `TYPE=` attribute supplies the browser with the means to determine how the linked file should be used. Browsers that do not support the specified MIME type will ignore the `<LINK>` tag. Internet Explorer 3.0 registers the text/css MIME type at the client during the installation of the browser software. This causes the `TYPE=` attribute to be ignored when the HTML file is read. You can, therefore, omit the `TYPE=` attribute when you are designing web pages to be read using Internet Explorer 3.0.

The `<LINK>` tag should be enclosed within the `<HEAD>` tags of the HTML document to which you will apply the styles. There is no need for a closing tag (for example, `</LINK>`). When specifying alternate style sheets, each should have its own individual `<LINK>` tag, complete with all the necessary attributes.

A browser is then able to construct a menu of alternate style sheets, possibly including additional reader styles stored at the client's location. Readers with special needs (for example, large type, and speech synthesis) can supply their own styles that can override the author's styles.

To see the effect of an external style sheet on an HTML file, open the sample file that you used to create the separate style sheet and delete the entire `<STYLE>` block. Insert a `<LINK>` element into the `<HEAD>` block like that shown that references your style sheet file in the `HREF=` attribute. When you open your sample file in Internet Explorer, it appears just as it did when the embedded styles were present.

Explorer Support When styles are linked, the document should appear just as it did when they were embedded, but in some ways it probably won't. Internet Explorer 3.0 has problems with certain style properties when they are used in external style sheets; for example, the `background` property. Backgrounds defined in linked style sheets are ignored when a linked style sheet is applied to the document, as are graphic image backgrounds in embedded styles.

USING THE *@IMPORT* FUNCTION

The @import function, defined in the CSS1 standard, is another method of linking style sheets to HTML documents. It is designed for use when style sheets are to be automatically applied to the document, without any interactive selection from the reader (as with <LINK>).

The syntax of the @import function is included within the <STYLE> tags, along with any embedded styles for that document. A typical example would appear as follows:

```
<STYLE>
@import url(http://www.mycorp.com/styles/
sheet1.css);
P      {font-size: 16}
</STYLE>
```

Specify multiple style sheets by using individual @import declarations, one after another. The contents of the style sheets are applied according to the order in which they are listed.

 **TIP** **Conflicting Styles**. Sometimes styles from different sources provide conflicting values for the same properties. This is a complex subject and the order of precedence defined by the CSS1 standard is discussed in Lesson 20.

In this lesson, you learned how to create a style sheet file and apply it to an HTML document. In the next lesson, you learn how to apply inline styles to specific document elements.

19

USING INLINE STYLE CODES

In this lesson, you learn how to apply style properties directly to individual HTML elements.

In previous lessons, you learned many different methods for isolating HTML elements in order to apply styles to them. Class, contextual, and ID selectors all have their uses and are an important part of the standard, but sometimes using them is inconvenient.

Styles provide you with effects that cannot be duplicated using conventional HTML codes, and there will be times when you want to apply one of these effects to a single text element in a quick and dirty manner. The CSS1 standard permits you to do this by allowing the use of STYLE as an attribute as well as an element.

This is referred to as applying *inline* styles because the style definitions are intermingled with the document contents, instead of being stored in a separate block or file. Inline styles override the effect of any embedded or linked style rules for the same selector. You could conceivably elect to apply all of your style definitions inline because the properties and values are identical to those used in embedded and linked styles. The excessive use of inline styles, however, essentially defeats the primary purpose for using styles in the first place.

Inline style properties are applied only to the text enclosed within the tags containing the properties. There are therefore no selectors for inline styles, as they can only address a single element. If the same effect is required elsewhere in the same document, the entire style attribute must be reproduced in another tag. This can add considerably to the size of your documents and make the HTML code much more difficult to decipher and maintain. Styles containing many different properties can be rather long when strung along a single line of text.

USING THE *STYLE* ATTRIBUTE

To apply an inline style, add an attribute called STYLE= to any normal HTML tag. The equal sign is followed by quotation marks that contain all of the properties and values that you want to assign to that tag, separated by semicolons in the usual manner. No curly brackets are used in inline styles. If you apply the style for the <P> tag from your **SAMPLE2.HTML** as an inline style, for example, it appears as follows:

```
<P STYLE="font-family: Verdana; font-size: 14pt;
margin-left: .1in; margin-right: .1in; color: navy">
```

Of course, you would have to insert exactly the same tag for every paragraph that you wanted to format.

The quotation marks replace the curly braces used in embedded and linked styles, and enclose the declaration to separate it from the rest of the tag. You can add any other attributes that you wish to a tag containing styles because the style syntax is fully compliant with the HTML standard.

> **TIP**
> **Syntax Deviation**   When creating inline styles, it is not necessary to enclose font family names that include spaces in quotation marks. They can interfere with the proper processing of the HTML tag.

Inline styles can chiefly be seen as an expedient way to apply the new effects defined by the CSS1 standard to an existing HTML document. If the web author does not have the time or inclination to plan the strategy by which embedded or linked styles are most effectively used, inline styles provide a quick alternative.

When you are working on existing HTML documents, keep in mind that inline styles can be particularly effective when you use them with the <DIV> and <SPAN> tags discussed in Lesson 6. With this combination, you can apply style effects to your pages without affecting your existing HTML code, or the appearance of your pages in a browser that does not support style sheets.

The ancestral inheritance rules of embedded styles are equally applicable to inline styles. The Verdana `font-family` value applied to the <P> tag in the previous sample, for example, overrides a different typeface specified in its parent element, regardless of whether the parent's properties are defined by inline or embedded styles.

The rules that govern the application of conflicting styles are a different matter. You can apply both inline and embedded (and even linked) styles within the same document. The issue of what happens when linked styles, embedded styles, and inline styles specify properties for the same selectors is decided by different guidelines, as covered in Lesson 20.

In this lesson, you learned how to use the STYLE attribute to create inline styles that are added directly to HTML tags. In the next lesson, you learn about the cascading effect of conflicting style definitions.

CASCADING STYLE PRECEDENCE

*In this lesson, you learn how to mix style types
effectively by examining the relationship between linked, embedded,
and inline styles in the same document.*

There are many scenarios in which you might want to create web
pages that use a combination of linked, embedded, and inline
styles. For example, you might have a collection of styles that
reflect the overall look of your web site, but you want to override
them in certain circumstances. Because modifying the style sheet
would affect other documents as well, it is preferable to code your
exceptions using embedded or inline styles.

In such situations, you will inevitably have style rules that con-
flict. A linked style sheet and an embedded style block may both
have rules for the <P> tag, which specify different values for the
same property.

The CSS1 standard's general rule is: Linked styles are overridden
by embedded styles and embedded styles are overridden by inline
styles. This is known as the system of *cascading* styles.

Explorer Support   Internet Explorer 3.0 violates the most
basic concept of cascading styles by allowing linked style
sheets to retain precedence over embedded styles. Inline
styles, however, do override linked ones.

This can easily be demonstrated by taking your **SAMPLE2.HTML**
file (shown following), and adding some inline styles to the body
of the document. The values of the inline properties override
those specified in either embedded or linked styles.

```
<HTML>
<HEAD>
<STYLE>
<!--
BODY      {font-size: 11pt;
           margin-left: 0in;
           background: black}

TD          {background: URL(\windows\Black Thatch.bmp)}

H2        {font-size: 24pt;
           font-family: Arial;
           text-align: center;
           color: red}

P         {font-family: Verdana;
           font-size: 14pt
           margin-left: .1in;
           margin-right: .1in;
           color: white}

.first    {margin-right: 50%;
           line-height: 16pt;
           text-align: right}

.second   {margin-left: 50%;
           line-height: 16pt;
           text-align: left}

.third    {margin-left: 25%;
           margin-right: 25%;
           line-height: 16pt;
           text-align: center}
-->
</STYLE>
</HEAD>
```

```
<BODY>
<CENTER>
<TABLE WIDTH=90% BORDER=none>
<TD>
<H2>HTML Style Sheets</H2>
<P CLASS=first>HTML style sheets are innovative primarily in
that they allow various different styles to be applied to web
pages by the author. Indeed, it could be said that all web
browsers already use a style to display text.</P>
<P CLASS=second>A style is simply a collection of text and
layout attributes that can be selectively applied to all or
part of a document. The idea of grouping them into a style
allows the author to easily apply the same collection of
attributes to many different parts of a document.</P>
<P CLASS=third>The HTML styles</SPAN> in Microsoft's Internet
Explorer 3.0 are based on a draft standard being developed by
the World Wide Web Consortium (W3C).</P>
</TD>
</TABLE>
</CENTER>
</BODY>
</HTML>
```

If, for example, you modify the <P CLASS=first> tag in the body
of the document to read <P CLASS=first STYLE="font-size:
18pt">, the 14-point text defined in the embedded style for the
<P> selector (shown in Figure 20.1) is replaced with the 18-point
text shown in Figure 20.2.

Notice, however, that while the text is displayed using the larger
font size, the other properties included in the same embedded
declaration remain in force. The inclusion of the STYLE= attribute
in an HTML tag does not override the entire embedded rule for
that tag, only the specific properties that are defined inline.

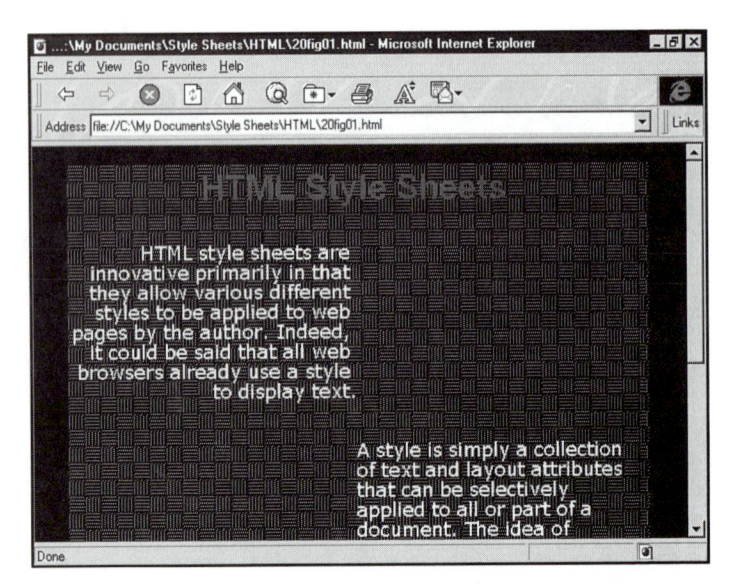

FIGURE 20.1 Properties defined in embedded style blocks modify the appearance of all the elements to which they are applied.

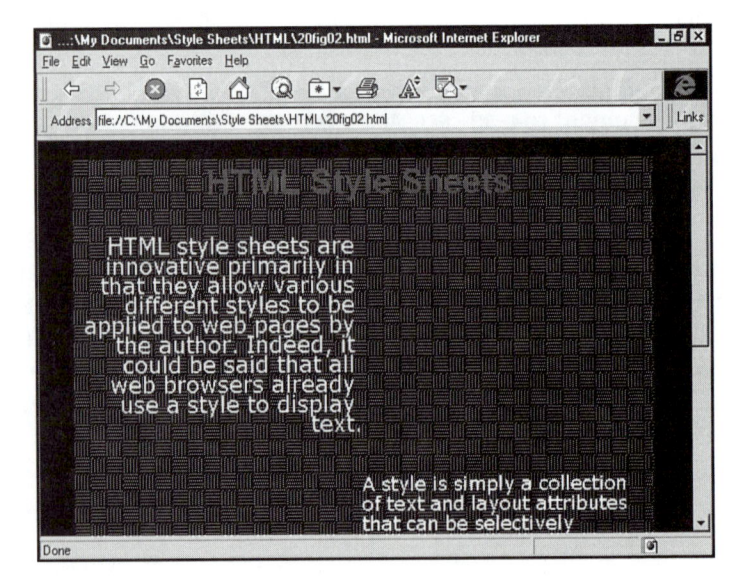

FIGURE 20.2 Properties included in specific HTML tags as inline styles affect only that element, and override the embedded properties.

ASSIGNING RULE PRIORITY

Apart from the three style types, you must consider the relationship between the author and the reader. In the future, it will be possible for readers to maintain personal style sheets that accommodate their own special needs. The general rule is that authors' styles take precedence over readers' styles that take precedence over the styles set in the browser.

There definitely are times when exceptions to this rule must be allowed, such as when a reader uses a style to provide large type or speech synthesis to compensate for a handicap.

The CSS1 standard calls for the use of a priority flag for this purpose. All rules are assigned a normal priority by default, but when a declaration is modified by the addition of an exclamation point and a priority indicator as shown, its default changes.

```
P       {font-size: 24pt ! important}
```

This priority rule will be used instead of any normal priority rule for the <P> tag, even in cases where it would be overridden under other circumstances. Thus, a person with vision difficulties could include rules of this type in a personal style sheet and have them take precedence over the authors' styles that are supplied with web pages.

UNDERSTANDING RULE PRECEDENCE

The cascading precedence is more complex than the basic relationship between linked, embedded, and inline styles. The CSS1 standard defines an algorithm which accounts for all of the factors discussed earlier and assigns them relative priorities.

To determine which rule for a particular selector should be applied when conflicts exist, examine the following conditions in the order in which they are listed:

- **Priority**   Rules assigned an important priority always take precedence over those with normal priority.

- **Style Origin**   An author's styles take precedence over the reader's styles, which take precedence over the browser's internal styles.

- **Style Type**   Inline styles take precedence over embedded styles, which take precedence over linked styles.

- **Specificity**   Selectors that are more specific take precedence over those that are more general. Specificity is computed by assigning a 3-digit number to each selector composed of the number of ID attributes in the selector (first digit), the number of classes in the selector (second digit), and the number of tag names in the selector (third digit). The selector with the highest number is awarded precedence. For example, a linked style using a simple class selector would have a value of 010. If an embedded style was defined for that same element using an ID selector, its value would be 100. The embedded style would therefore take precedence.

- **Style Order**   All other factors being equal, the rule specified last should take precedence.

This algorithm takes factors into account that do not apply to the practical applications of HTML style sheets as they stand today. The Cascading Style Sheets document is still a draft standard. A good deal of work has to be done before the standard is complete and even more before it is realized in commercial products that make all of the standard's potential a reality.

The time factor for standards developments, however, has taken a radically different turn in the last two years. Standards that at one time would require years of study and refinement are now being completed in a matter of months. Product cycles for Internet related technologies have accelerated enormously to the point that testing of new versions begins almost immediately after the release of the old ones.

In less than a year, style sheets will be part of a browser's standard equipment. In the future, the use of styles will not be an optional feature, so the time to begin learning their intricacies is now.

WINDOWS AND INTERNET EXPLORER TRUETYPE FONT SAMPLES

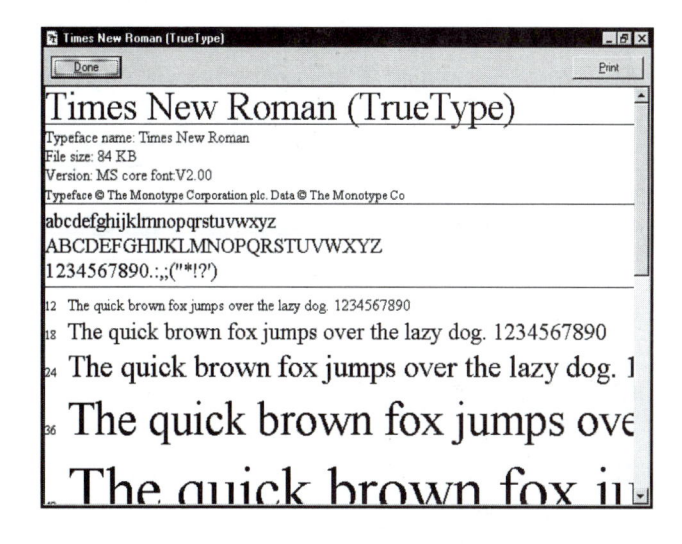

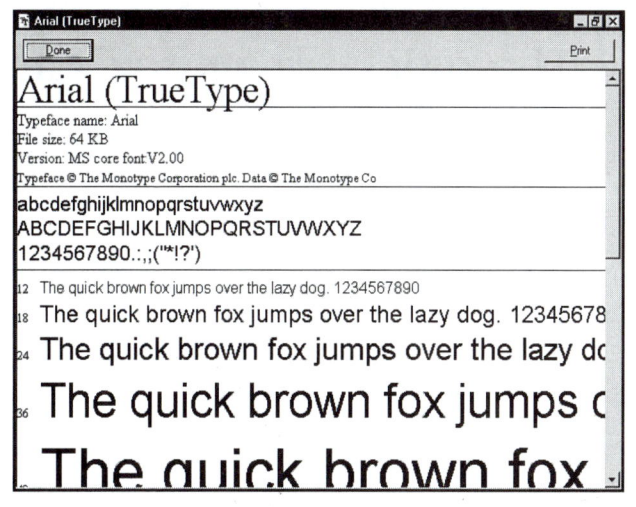

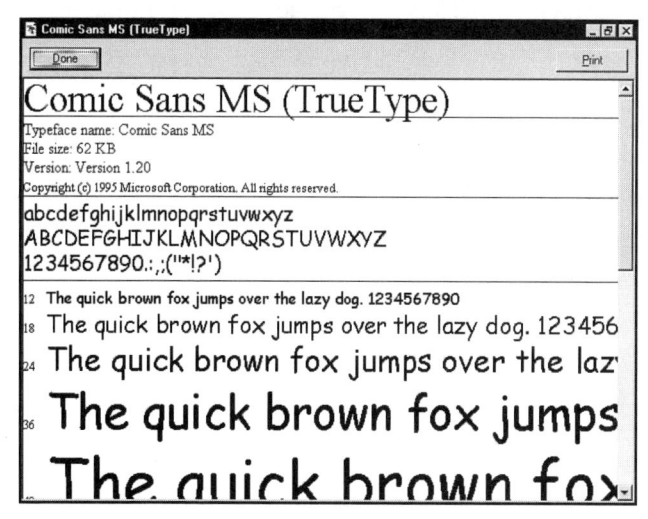

B

STYLE SHEET PROPERTIES QUICK REFERENCE

PROPERTY	DESCRIPTION	VALUES
font	Groups `font-family`, `font-size`, `font-weight`, `font-style`, and `line-height` properties	
font-family	Selects the typeface	font names
font-size	Selects the type size	points (pt) inches (in) centimeters (cm) pixels (px) ems (em) percentages xx-large x-large large medium small x-small xx-small larger smaller
font-weight	Selects type thickness	extra-bold bold demi-bold medium demi-light light extra-light bolder lighter

PROPERTY	DESCRIPTION	VALUES
font-style	Applies special font effects	none italic oblique small-caps
text-decoration	Applies special font effects that are created in the browser	none effects underline overline line-through
line-height	Applies leading	points (pt) inches (in) centimeters (cm) pixels (px) ems (em) percentages
letter-spacing	Adjusts space between letters	points (pt) inches (in) centimeters (cm) pixels (px) ems (em) percentages
word-spacing	Adjusts space between words	points (pt) inches (in) centimeters (cm) pixels (px) ems (em) percentages
color	Applies color to text	black navy blue aqua purple maroon green red

continues

continued

Property	Description	Values

		gray
		fuchsia
		teal
		lime
		yellow
		white
		olive
		silver
		#xxx (hex)
		#xxxxxx (hex)
		RGB(x,x,x)(dec)
		RGB(x,x,x) (%)

background	Applies color or image	same as above URL (url) repeat no-repeat repeat-x repeat-y fixed scroll points (pt) inches (in) centimeters (cm) pixels (px) ems (em) percentages
margin	Groups values for margin-top, margin-bottom, margin-left, and margin-right	
margin-bottom margin-top margin-left margin-right	Specifies margin size	points (pt) inches (in) centimeters (cm) pixels (px) ems (em) percentages

PROPERTY	DESCRIPTION	VALUES
padding	Specifies distance between content and border	points (pt) inches (in) centimeters (cm) pixels (px) ems (em) percentages
border	Groups values for border-bottom, border-top, border-left, border-right	
border-bottom border-top border-left border-right	Specifies border attributes	thin medium thick points (pt) inches (in) centimeters (cm) pixels (px) ems (em) colors URL (url)
text-indent	Specifies paragraph indent	points (pt) amount inches (in) centimeters (cm) pixels (px) ems (em) percentages
text-align	Specifies justification	left right center justify
text-transform	Adjusts text capitalization	capitalize uppercase lowercase none

GLOSSARY

absolute value—A measurement using a concrete scale such as points, inches, or centimeters; the opposite of a relative value.

attribute—A parameter that can be added to an HTML tag to alter or enhance its purpose. For example, the WIDTH= attribute can be added to the <HR> to specify the length of a horizontal rule, in the form <HR WIDTH=50%>.

block element—An HTML element that is automatically preceded and followed by a line feed in the client browser (for example, <P> or <H1>); opposite of an inline element.

body—The part of an HTML document that contains the actual content that displays in the client's browser; the part of an HTML document contained within the <BODY> and </BODY> tags.

border—The rectangular line surrounding the contents of an element; the dividing line between the padding and the margin.

canvas—The entire area of the web browser window in which HTML documents are displayed.

class selector—A means to isolate specific HTML tags for the application of styles by the addition of the CLASS= attribute.

contextual selector—A means to isolate specific HTML tags for the application of styles by specifying their exact location in relation to other HTML tags.

cursive—A font that resembles a calligraphic longhand, except that the letters are distinctly separated.

declaration—Part of a style rule consisting of a property and its associated value.

element—The part of a document that is enclosed between any pair of opening and closing HTML tags.

em—A unit of length corresponding to the width of a font's capital M at whatever size it is displayed.

font—In traditional printing, a typeface in a single size and a particular weight and style; in current usage, a typeface family in any size, weight, and style.

granularity—The degree to which like elements in an HTML document have had individual styles applied to them through the use of distinguishing selectors.

hanging indent—A text formatting expression defining a case when the first line of a block of text is extended to the left, beyond the rest of the paragraph.

hexadecimal—A counting system that uses 16 digits, traditionally notated as 0, 1, 2, 3, 4, 5, 6, 7, 8, 9, A, B, C, D, E, F.

inline element—An HTML element that does not cause the addition of preceding and following line feeds in the client browser (for example, <STRONG> or <I>); opposite of a block element.

justification—The alignment of text in relation to the left and right margins containing it.

kerning—The adjustment of the white space left between specific pairs of letters to account for the architectural design of the typeface.

leading—The white space between an element's lines of text.

margin—The white space surrounding an element's rectangular border.

padding—The white space between and element's border and the contents itself.

point—A unit of measurement used in printing and publishing equal to 1/72 inch.

property—Part of a style that is used to define a particular aspect of an element's appearance or location.

pseudo-class—A means of selecting certain text in an HTML document, based not on the HTML code of the document itself, but on other external conditions applied by the web browser.

pseudo-element—A term used to identify a portion of another element according to the way it is displayed by a particular web browser configuration.

relative value—A measurement that is based on a comparison to another measurement, such as a percentage; opposite of absolute value.

rule—Part of a style sheet consisting of a selector and one or more declarations.

sans serif—A typeface in which the letters do not have small decorative ends; opposite of serif.

selector—Part of a rule indicating the element(s) to which the style should be applied.

serif—A typeface in which the letters have small decorative ends, such as those that descend from the ends of the crossbar on the letter T; opposite of sans serif.

style—A collection of properties and their values that are used to modify the appearance or location of HTML elements on a web page.

tracking—The amount of white space left between letters and words in a block of text.

typeface—An alphabet of a unified design used for publishing documents by mechanical or digital means.

value—A declaration of the specific way in which a property is to be applied to the selected element(s).

white space—Any part of a document not covered by images or text (whether or not the background of the page is actually white).

INDEX

V

values
background property, inserting, 116
keyword, defining, 107
negative margin, 80-83
optional, 101
relative, 20-21
relative font size, 58-61
RGB (red, green, and blue) value, 108-111
text-decoration property, inheriting, 72

variants
defining, 66
fonts (typestyle), 64-66

Verdana font, 134, 144
viewing
online fonts, 45
properties, 123

W-Z

watermark technique, 120
web browsers, default browser style, 3-4
web pages
color palette, 110
color property, 106-110

creating, 8-10
fonts, 47
ID selector, 37-38
inheritance, 42
pseudo-classes, 121
relative values, 59
style sheets, inserting, 6-7
styles, 1
text-transform properties, 72
third-generation selectors, 32-36
TYPE attribute, 34

weights, fonts, 66-67
white spaces, 4
letter-spacing properties, 97-98
line-height property, enlarging, 96
organizing, 92-98
properties, word-spacing, 92-97

Windows 95 fonts, 46-47
Windows NT fonts, 46-47
word-spacing property, 96-97, 145
workarounds, design, 5